ACKNOWLEDGMENTS

I wish to acknowledge the incalculable contribution of the faculty at the University of Arizona in giving me the academic tools with which to understand, confront and defy traditions and circumstances that were detrimental and confining. In order of appearance: Dr. Christopher Carroll, Dr. Susan White, Debra White-Stanley, Dr. Laura Berry, Dr. William Epstein, Dr. Fred Keifer, Dr. Roger Bowen, Dr. John Warnock, Dr. Charlie Bertsch, Bibiana Law, Wendy Thomas, Dr. Peter Medine, Dr. Charles Scruggs, Deborah, Michelle, Marsha, Joann Rockwell, Jeff Artzi. More than the professors, it was often my fellow students who gave me faith in my abilities and potential to succeed. To my classmates and intellectual companions who became so much more than that, "Thank you for your friendship."

To my good friend Bianca Lehman, who encouraged me to return to school, gave me advice, listened to me cry and gave me a place at her kitchen table to feel safe and reconnoiter; I can never repay the gift of her friendship.

To Tama and Michael White, my editor and production advisor, whose support, wise advice, loving and respectful relationship were an unexpected gift and inspiration in such tumultuous times. They believed in *The House of Many Faces* before anyone else and often gave me the faith to forge ahead with the conviction that others whom I respected, were as passionate about what I was trying to achieve as I was. Jane Candia Coleman, thank you for saying, "This is beautiful and I congratulate you. I will help you in any way I can." What new author could hope to hear such sweet words?

To Thom Sherwood, who listened to what I asked for and translated the book I saw in my mind into the artifact that I, and others, could hold in their hands. Once again, because of a gifted artisan, a beautiful object evolved to disguise the harsh reality hidden within.

To my parents, who made me healthy and whole, who devoted their lives to me. Throughout it all, I knew that the foundation I built upon was the gift of their love. The conviction and strength to forge ahead came from a home where I was wanted and loved, from a family, parents, sister, aunts, uncles and cousins who loved me just because I was— myself.

To my children, Thano, Nicholas and Stephanie. You are the greatest treasures to enrich my life, the reason that this journey was meant to be. The question, "What did I teach you with my life?" was a litany and guide in so much of what I was, and what I will strive to be. My responsibility to you is to fulfill my potential with integrity and honour, because what I am will always reflect upon you.

And to Nacho. For whatever reason, my journey was meant to be a part of yours. I wish you well.

Konstantina Dimitra Mahlia
Tucson, Arizona
June 2004

Emma—
Thank you for
stopping by!
Konstantina
2007

READER'S COMMENTS

"Your personal, passionate voice is all lightning and thunder."

"The objectification and sexualization of a woman is a heavy wound— You gave the body power and grace."

"Thank you for putting your inner voice into the written word."

"My world will never be the same for having seen it through your eyes."

"Your clarity and bravery will inspire."

Concept and Design: Konstantina Dimitra Mahlia

Editing, Consultants: Michael & Tama White
Ghostriver Publications

Book Production and Typography: Thom Sherwood
COLORTEKS Creative

Illustration: Michael Santini

Printing: Arizona Lithographers

ISBN 0-9759925-0-3

The House of Many Faces

Non-Fiction Literature
First Edition

520.891.0553
mahlia_mallia@worldnet.att.net

the House of MANY FACES

KONSTANTINA DIMITRA MAHLIA

11
11
12
2
13
9
1
3
6
22
8
5
4
19
27
18
7
15
26
7
7
29
17
25
18
7
28
7
10
24
20
30
23
29
21
14
16
7
7
11
11

Frontispiece Key

The frontispiece is another medium with which to express a personal, even private message, as it "nourishes artistic endeavour both consciously and unconsciously."

1 .... Hill: state of full consciousness

2 .... Home: genesis of the memoir

3 .... Labyrinth: complex, personal journey to find oneself; anagnorisis

4&5 ... Daughter Truth, Father Time: two that always travel together, because, eventually justice is done when truth is revealed by time. Father Time also represents death, because in time, death will arrive to cut down life and cease the passage of time in earthly life.

6 .... Gate: threshold she has passed through. The gate is also the portal to the new life where she stands.

7 .... Flowers: traditional symbol of the impermanence of earthly life. Once picked, flowers shortly die. They also represent the author's love of the garden, the "hortus conclusus," a composition in constant flux. The garden also represents the human soul which must be cared for and cultivated. A garden should be place of peace, light and beauty, echoing the primordial perfection of nature. The garden is also a symbol of the "female principal," the author's sex, which defined many of the opportunities and choices given her.

8 .... Butterfly: symbol of transformation, beauty, hope and promise arising from the confinement of the chrysalis lying on the ground below.

9 .... Cupid: one who sits on top of the gate she has passed through. His work to romantically entrap her is done. Cupid not only represents romantic love, but the sinister love of mismatched couples.

10 ...... Snake: intelligence, knowledge and wisdom

11 ...... Laurel leaves: loyalty, honour and triumph, the berries, fruitful endeavour.

12 ...... The Eye of Providence: overseer of the whole journey

13 ...... The Sun: hope emerging from darker times

14 ...... Broken Tablet/Broken Crest: broken marital contract, the fractured partnership she strove for and never achieved

15 ...... The Woman: bowed head— weariness, her upright position— recovering strength, strength needed to move forward

16 ...... Skull: inevitable death and the vanity of her efforts

17 ...... Mirror: reflection of self knowledge, truth, self-realization, wisdom, the mind and the soul, the mirror of the universe and a reflection of the temporal world

18 ...... Two Columns: "testis temporus," the witness of time and "vita memorie," the life of memory. The break in the column represents fortitude.

19 ...... Three Bees: industry, diligence, order, sobriety, creativity and eloquence. In Greek tradition, the bee is said to represent the soul.

20 ...... Frog: the material goods which gain so much attention they obscure reality with their presence

21 ...... Stack of Books: love of knowledge and learning, the book aflame symbolizing the casting off of old traditions and beliefs

22 ...... Tree of Life: twelve types of fruit representing the rewards of spiritual growth, including wisdom, love, truth and beauty; the cluster of three plums represent her fidelity and independence from family and spouse. Lemon: faithful love; pear: hope; apple: temptation and salvation. The tree also represents growth and creative power; its vertical shape, an upward surge, conveys life, hope, goodness and health.

23 ...... Barefeet: connection to the real world, not the illusory one

24 ...... Footsteps: movement forward, not backwards, leaving the past to seek the promise of the future

25 ...... Nudity: her natural state as she came into the world, her nakedness symbolic of innocence and freedom

26 ...... Heart: understanding, love, courage, sorrow and joy in life. It is exposed because the heart represents the central wisdom of feeling as opposed to the head, wisdom of reason; both are intelligence, but the heart is also compassion, understanding and the secret place of love and charity because it contains life's blood.

27 ...... Crown: feathers and laurel leaves representing her Greek heritage and her North American birthplace

28 ...... Key: the key of fidelity

29 ...... Broken Cords: fate, time, limitation and the inescapable. The cords are broken to represent her break with the symbols they represent.

30 ...... Compass: intelligence, creativity and newfound direction

TABLE OF CONTENTS

PRELUDE

She sat on the terrace overlooking Nogales, the bright Arizona sun warming her skin, remembering how cold she had been that overcast day last January, the day after deciding she wanted a divorce. She had driven to Tucson with her daughter, the window rolled down, the cold air battering her face, whipping her hair, as she fought down the nausea that kept hitting her in waves. "He's going to get me," she kept thinking. When she was in the office of the counselor later that day, he had stared at her as she stood up and started pacing the room. "I've never seen you like this. What's going on?" "You don't understand. You don't know who you're dealing with. You've never seen that side of him. He doesn't show it to anyone but me. He will try to destroy me." "Who do you think that I deal with in this office? You think that I can't handle him?" She wanted to believe that there was someone who could protect her from her husband, but nobody ever had. They couldn't believe him to be the man that she had seen, the man who had pushed her into the wall, the man who had slapped her and dragged her up the stairs of her mother's house by her hair, the man who had stood in the door, drunk, and screamed at her, "Go to hell," the man who had pushed her across the room so hard that she had lost her balance, fallen and cracked her wrist. This was the man who had seen her dressed to go out, waiting for a compliment from him, and said instead, "You think that you look so great, don't you? You just want everyone to look at you. You look ugly." It had been one of her first steps at defending herself the time she had replied, "I hope you never say something like that to your daughter when she wants your approval." This was the same man who later said he was sorry, that he loved her, that it wouldn't happen again, the man who held her hand in the car and lifted it to his mouth to kiss it, to show his love of her. His love of her. Of her. Of Her. His Wife. His.

Life is strange, both joy and pain; the betrayal and the kiss.

They had been together in his car, again driving to see their counselor, when he had begun to taunt her, disparaging what she had to say; diminishing her. She had turned in a fury and begun to pummel his arm as he drove. "I hate you! You had no right to destroy my life. Why? Why me? What did I do to you? Stop the car! Stop the car!" And when he hadn't stopped, she had opened the door against the wind and tried to jump out.

Violence begets violence... as a battered child grows up to be an abuser, a battered animal awaits its chance to do unto others as has been done unto him.

He had slowed down in alarm when she almost fell out, slowing enough for her to catch her balance and start to stumble along even as the car had continued to move. He rolled down the window and paced the car next to her. "Get in the car! Get in the car!" "No! I won't get in the car with you." He had been apoplectic; she, determined to get away from him. She knew him well enough to know that he was afraid someone they knew would recognize them. He pulled over to park the car and get her. Alarmed, in high heels, she scrambled through the brush before he could get around the car and luckily found a gap in the barb wire fence that separated the frontage road from the highway. Squeezing through, she had walked as fast as she could with no clear idea of what would come next, desperate to avoid the pain of being in his company. She had seen the car turn around and knew that he would come and try to find her. Finding a culvert to hide in until he passed by, she scrambled to hide behind trash receptacles, bushes, around corners of houses every time his car would approach, until finally, he stopped looking for her. An old man in a beatup pickup truck must have seen what happened and came to investigate. He offered her a ride to the nearest town, glancing across at her tight face as they drove along without comment, his generous gesture inadequately repaid with a quiet, "Thank you," when she got out at the gas station a few miles down the road. Nobody had known of that day except the counselor.

Why's pain the only way to happiness?

Later, the counselor had contemplated her over his notebook, then said, "What makes you think that he won't divorce you?" She had returned his look and matter of factly replied, "He won't divorce me. Then he wouldn't own me anymore. In his mind, love is ownership, and I am his. Forever. That's the pathology of his jealousy, the fear that someone else could have me, touch me, want me, even look at me."

He repeated pensively to himself his fatal sentence: "No one shall have her."

Months later her son would say to her, "But he's crazy about you, don't you see?" She had studied him as she thought, without speaking, "Exactly. It's not a healthy love. It's crazy and cruel and hurtful. That's not love. Not to me. I want something else." She finally came up with the metaphor of a beautiful, brightly coloured butterfly, a creature born to be free, born to bring beauty to the world, as analogous to her situation. He had seen this butterfly and wanted it to be his, so he had captured it and put it under a glass dome where he, and he alone, could watch it and enjoy it. No one else was to see it. It was his.

I promise you you'll see the sun again.

But he was afraid that the butterfly would fly off and leave him, so he took the butterfly and pulled off its wings, one at a time, so that it could never leave. He had destroyed what he loved. That was what his love had done. He later said to a friend, who told her mother, "My problem was that I loved her too much."

> **Because of her, because of her.**

She strove to correct the imbalance, to create a world where she could survive. She felt that she wasn't alone in trying to escape her reality. She saw others who used money, sex, drugs, social status, food, drinking, self injury, and, as she did, the world of art and illusions, to sustain a struggle for equilibrium and find escape from the pain of their existence.

> **In art man lives outside of himself, outside of his burdens, the burdens of life. Every creative, artistic act is a partial transfiguration of life**

Her own mind, her inclination to constantly analyze the elements of destruction gave her no quarter. Her reality was a raw wound that seemed destined to consume her. So she sustained herself by withdrawing, hiding from the pain in a beautiful house, a gracious home where she could shroud the truth, disguising it to her own psyche until finally trusting the world by relinquishing the burden of deception. By divulging her bottled up, personal life the pain began to devour itself. Instead of consuming her soul, it was blown away as though ashes after the fierce, painful inferno that had left her scathed but alive. She too was everyman, the human experience was her own as well, feelings and thoughts echoed in her art, telling the truth while seducing one and all into the realm of a beautiful, soothing, illusion.

> **The mind must withdraw from reality and create a world of artificial perfection. Human nature desires a utopian world.**

Chapter ONE

The Mantlepiece

She approached the scrolled, wrought-iron gate of the courtyard. Passing through the gates hung between two roughly plastered pillars, she glanced up at the stone ball finials that capped the columns and the flanking cypress trees overshadowing her head. On the far side of the creaking gate, a small verdant garden was protected by the elegant, towering north face of the house.

The garden is a representation of Paradise, "a place of peace, light, and beauty, echoing the primordial perfection of nature."

The entrance to the house should have been imposing, but the enclosed space covered in creeping fig was an inviting portal that greeted all who approached. As the ivy curled over the door's pocked stone frame, its delicate filigree of spade-shaped leaves and gnarled branches lovingly clung to the rough plaster walls in a harmonious partnership. She let the scent, the light and the soft sounds of the garden play over her as she stood in the portico of the house, pensive as she studied the two, great, grey weathered doors studded with bronze escutcheons. She touched a fingertip to the bronze face of a woman and man staring outwards, standing sentry.

> **The house at its threshold gives evidence of the master's good will.**

The face of Demeter and Hercules created allegorical symbols of her own union. The male wore a cape, a lion's pelt, his kill, to symbolize his position as the defender of the home and guardian of the house. His expression showed him ready to deter those who approached his woman or his home. The woman's gentle face was wreathed in grape leaves and vines to symbolize the feminine attributes of fertility and the gentle, steadfast love that the woman of this home would provide.

> **Strength is chiefly valued in the male and comliness in the female.**

Entering, she shut the door behind her. The two faces looked out, stoic sentinels and perpetual guardians keeping the world at bay and her within. The beauty eased her spirit as she pushed open the heavy door, admitting her to the world she had created. This vestibule was a barrier that protected her home from uninvited entry. Above the doors hung a copper engraving she had bought in a small antique shop. The image was of an earlier time, of a young couple sitting together in a simple room in front of their hearth. They looked content, the young woman handing their infant over to her smiling husband. It had seemed to appropriately symbolize what a home was, illustrating how for a man and woman of any society it was the beginning of a new generation, a new bloodline. This was what matrimony was meant to produce in any culture: union, offspring, hearth and home. Their image had created a yearning in her for the moments of contentment which in her own marriage had been so rare. It hung as a promise of what could be.

She stepped up into the living room, a space luminous with gentle, northern light. Ivory, limestone tiles, roughly textured, cream-coloured walls and dark, heavy, beams created a neutral backdrop to enhance the composition of the room, rather than compete with it. The space she had created both invited and soothed her. It was good. The anchor in the room was the grey stone fireplace with its corbels of acanthus leaves and its regal medallion.

We shape our dwellings and afterwards our dwellings shape us.

When they had married, she had looked through the history books for something befitting their union. Her mother's family and his father's were from the same territory in Greece, close to the ancient foundations of Mycenae. The coinage of the ancient city-state had been her inspiration and had become the two lion's bodies facing one another, two bodies joined by one head, their front paws resting on an anvil. She had made a medallion for Nacho from that symbol and engraved it with the words,

"Forever to be three, you and I and we Never again separate, but always as one."

The symbol in the medallion had later become a ring for him with a carved bloodstone and then a ring for her and for each of their three children. The crest had become their family emblem, their seal, their family promise. Three people had descended from a union of two, three lives forever linking the two of them more irrevocably than stone, gold, promises, love or wedding vows ever would.

The fireplace was flanked by two old bureaus that were illuminated by a pair of bronze lamps, one a hunched woodsman hard at work, one his wife gathering the fruit of his labour. Above them hung two paired tapestries of forested landscapes, the woven composition of old trees in a pastoral setting reflecting the woodcutter's origins, as the lions reflected her own. Two sofas faced each other in front of the fireplace, mirrored by two oversized chairs in cream suede. Pairs of soft down cushions covered in beige and camel silk, suede and velvet created downy islands of comfort. The center cushions of each sofa had been embroidered for her by her mother, the one of a male, the other of a female pug elegantly attired in bright, medieval court dress and jewels. She stood enveloped by the aura of the room she had created and she knew that it was good.

Beauty was given to him at birth. Beauty was the capacity to see beauty, to select the beautiful from the beautiful.

The sofas, the chairs, the bureaus, the lamps, the tapestries, the huge pots of dried hydrangeas on the mantlepiece, the two antique majolica plates with their pastel hues and delicate arabesques hung over the double French doors that led to the balastered balcony outside the living room pleased her. Each element had its companion. The room was full of couplings. The female and the male, the couple, the pair, were the metaphoric origin of everything in the room. She realized now that for most of her life, she too had seen everything as being part of a couple, a part of a half. A chair for her, a chair for him, a door for her, a door for him, a lamp for her, a lamp for him— this was the harmony she had intended to create: balance in composition. They were supposed to have become a "we" on that day they married, but everything she had created to inspire the "we" hadn't been enough. The symbol of their union, the two bodies with one head, had been an illusion, a promise of what could have been, but that never was.

> The perfection of illusion was also the hour of disillusionment.

The consol she had designed with the young woman's face carved in golden wood, the gilt-framed picture above it, the gay features in the painting above the Boule chest, all told her another tale, the story of an alliance she had created, passages of rite. The console's single face was that of Giulietta— there was no Romeo; the painting hanging above it depicted an old woman teaching a young girl her role in life. The portrait above the Boule chest was of a girl in the prime of her youth, ready for marriage though barely a woman. She looked with surprise at each piece, then once again at the collage she had instinctively created by collecting the stages of a woman's life with these pieces, in this room that was also so much a statement about the "we" in her journey. The child, the young girl, the young woman in love, the young woman ready to marry, the mother, the crone; they were all there. There was no permanence in their images, there was no forever in their stories, they weren't part of a whole, but rather illustrated the inevitable evolution of a woman's journey, each age a part of the female cycle.

> Intellect is delighted by design, only in those whose very nature draws them to it, without guidance of a master.

But there was one image, a painting that hung alone, facing the room. It was of herself. She had commissioned it when she turned thirty to mark another milestone in her life, the closure of a decade, the end of her childbearing, the end of her innocence. She had wanted the portrait painted as an anniversary gift for Nacho, her husband, a memento to mark their tenth anniversary. He hadn't liked it and had never explained his obvious resentment when she had gifted it to him. "It doesn't look like you," had been his explanation, but she had known it to be more than that. It had been a portrait of her as the artist had seen her— a woman that stood alone. The young woman, facing forward, looked out of the canvas and off into the distance. Long after she lived, those who saw this image would know her name; it would not be lost as long as the canvas remained, giving it a title. A single word was carved in the painted stone wall: her name, Konstantina.

> **Put into this soul a fierce thirst for beauty — to know it, to create it; to be something—**

She had sat for the painter for days, knowing that in great part the outcome of the portrait depended upon her participation. Until then, she had been the "silent partner" in her marriage, and part of her husband's resentment of her portrait may have been due to the fact that her image established her position in their home— a place that he alone should have held as head of the house, and one that her portrait threatened. Banks, buildings, offices— even his own, had portraits of their founding fathers hanging on their walls. Not a woman, not in his world.

> **"Dwindle into a wife."**

She had wanted that portrait to establish her position as matriarch of this family, as a woman who had a position of authority and respect in her home and as a keepsake for her children. She had wanted to establish that her influence in their lives was just as important as the person who provided for their financial needs. She had wanted to say what she couldn't say aloud, that she was their mother, the parent whose surname they didn't carry forward, but whose lineage would be perpetrated in them with her blood. "This was what she looked like in the prime of her life. This woman was our mother. This woman gave us life and her unconditional love every day that she had breath in her body."

> **She was a woman, with her instinctive fears, her inexplicable whims, her bravado, her defiance, and her delicious delicacy of feeling.**

"This woman gave me her love and chose me as her spouse," was what she wanted Nacho to say. She imagined him thinking, "She always wanted to be more, she always wanted more than I was, more than I had to give. She is mine, but I can't hold her, she won't let me. She always wants to go somewhere and be something that is not where I can see her all the time. I hate it, I hate it that I don't know where she is all the time, what's she's doing, who's she with. If she would only stay home."

Her face looked out of the canvas, away to a place unseen, with an easy gaze of quiet strength that had surprised her when she had seen the finished portrait, surprised that the artist had seen that quality in her. She looked steady and sure of where she was going at a time when she hadn't felt defined in who she was or what she could do. The woman in the painting was a portrait of what the artist had seen, a woman who was not very young, but not yet middle-aged, a woman standing alone with only a simple flower in the hand that rested on a plain stone wall, with her dark hair swept up, a few curls slipping down against her neck. She was dressed in a white dress that bared her shoulders, fitted close to her body in a figure framed against a soft blue sky that spoke of sun and warmth, fresh, sweet air and a horizon without boundaries.

> Cogito ergo sum
> I think therefore I am.

But even as she turned, a shadow waited for her in the corner of the room. She could see a woman huddled in her nightgown, sitting on the cold, stone tiles, barefoot, crying, her head bowed to muffle her tears so that no one could hear her, so that the footsteps walking through the house, echoing through the rooms, wouldn't find her. The house was a trap. In order to escape, she would be discovered, so she stayed, quiet, trembling, as the footsteps neared. "What are you doing? What's wrong with you? Look at you. You're freezing. Get up."

The shadow slowly dissolved as she turned away. That woman was a shadow, a ghost, a woman who had discovered her strength and substance to give herself form. She was indefatigable in her mission to create strength and power and never submit, never, never submit. That was why her image was strong; it was the essence of her.

> **Our house had a heart, and a soul, and eyes to see us with; and approvals and solicitudes, and deep sympathies; it was of us, and we were in its confidence, and lived in its grace and in the peace of its benediction... We could not enter it unmoved.**

Chapter TWO

The Photograph

As she passed by the gleaming dark wood of the Mexican-Chippendale bureau as she did many times a day, the round frame of Mexican silver in the back of the group of family photos caught her eye. The faded black-and-white image of a serious, balding, round faced, middle-aged man in a black suit looked out of the frame. It was an old, formal picture of her Greek father-in-law from the nineteen-twenties. It was the only picture of him in the collection of photographs. He had died months before she married. She picked up the frame in her hand and as she contemplated his image, she remembered how he had looked in the casket the day of his funeral. It had been the first time she had seen a dead body, and her fiancée, Nacho, had encouraged her to touch his dead father's face.

The rest is silence.

The first time she had met this man, she had been fifteen and he had been the same age as her grandfather, old enough to be her father's father. A tall man even as he hunched with his age, he had been well over six feet tall with huge hands and feet. She had spoken to him infrequently, in short conversations, in the years before she and Nacho made a commitment to one another, only knowing that he approved of her for his son. He had died before she could get to know this man, her husband loved, adored and respected. He had been the patriarch of the family and now he was dead.

> All human things are subject to decay
>
> And when fate summons
>
> Monarchs must obey.

There had been so much to absorb in that short frame of time twenty-two years ago. It had been a "baptism by fire" as she struggled to stay on her feet, literally, stunned by everything she was bombarded with that was foreign and unfamiliar to her. It had been a forty-eight hour baptism into a culture that was not her own, as she adapted as quickly as she could to this new world, a Mexican world, with only her Anglo and Greek heritage as guide rails. In a situation where established guidelines, her own traditions, were all she had to keep her on track, hers had been made of "silly putty." Instead of being on a solid bridge, she was pushed onto a suspension bridge of wobbly, fragile rope and broken wood planks connecting her from one world to the next. Her father-in-law to be had died, and she had had to adapt quickly to the circumstances and customs that were her new frame of reference.

She had never been to a funeral before her father-in-law died. He had been seventy-four to her twenty and not technically her father-in-law yet. He was supposed to have become that at Nacho's and her wedding three months later on June the fourteenth. It had been March the second and he had just died of pancreatic cancer. She hadn't seen Nacho cry. It had been a devastatingly quick degeneration from the time of diagnosis to death two weeks later, and as the fianceé, it had been expected that she participate as a family member. But she wasn't. As she had watched Nacho experience this tremendously painful loss, there had been so many things that she questioned, so much that was unfamiliar, so much that she couldn't relate to as she dealt with many new and foreign experiences too.

They had told them only that morning that he only had hours

left to live. He wasn't conscious. The eldest sister, the oldest of the children, was arriving from Mexico with her husband. She was to go with Nacho to the airport to pick them up. She and Nacho both knew that there was a chance they wouldn't make it back in time, but Nacho was the second son, the middle son of the family, the "courier," the "go between"... and his father's favorite. The eldest son should have been the favorite, but he wasn't. Nacho should have been with his father, but he was the one sent off, because he wasn't the eldest, because it was his place to do what was asked of him without question. Because.

Driving back from the airport the tension in the car had been palpably oppressive. As Nacho drove the car through the hospital parking lot to the access door outside his father's room, they could see the eldest son outside crying, his head bowed to his chest. It was too late. Nacho parked the car and walked into the hospital. She hurried to catch up, but he had disappeared by the time she got to the door. Seven children, sons-in-law, grandchildren and friends were gathered in clusters grieving, crying and holding on to one another. Nacho wasn't there. She tried to behave appropriately, but her feelings were not the same as theirs. She had hardly known him. How could she share what they felt because of her relationship to the son? She felt sad, she felt sorry for all of them, but she didn't feel sad inside; yet, in that moment, she was considered to be one of them. In that moment, they included her, enveloping her in their sorrow, tying her to their traditions.

Funeral arrangements had to be made. She knew that Nacho's father had expressed a desire to be buried in Tucson by a Greek priest in the cemetery where many of his friends lay. "No." Nachos' mother had decreed that he was to be buried in Mexico. "But aren't the wishes of the dead respected here?" she had asked Nacho. "He made it very clear that he wanted to be buried here." "But my mother wants him to be buried in Mexico. She's alive and he's not. What does it matter what he wanted? He's dead now. What's more important is that we follow her wishes." But she had known that she had made him uncomfortable by her questions. He hadn't wanted to doubt his mother. He was used to doing as he was told. That was his way to show respect, to do as he was told.

She hadn't understood. It had gone against everything she knew about respect, not to honour the wishes of the dead even after they were gone. They didn't understand her and she didn't understand them. She saw them as being 'bad,' they didn't understand what was wrong.

> **I have become a kind of "enfant terrible" in my new homeland, due to my inability to keep silent and to swallow everything that happens here.**

The body had to be shipped down to Mexico. Papers and document after document were produced; shipping, exporting, death certificates processed. They had needed a cargo plane for the body. Who would go with the body? How was the rest of the family going to get there? There were over twenty people to make travel arrangements for and a corpse. She had just waited to be where they wanted her when they wanted her. It had felt so disorganized and chaotic. What was she to wear? What did they think was appropriate? How long would she be there? She knew that they had a lot of rules that were unfamiliar to her and she had to catch up quickly.

"What are you wearing? That's not appropriate. Find something to the knee and long-sleeved, black, navy or grey. No pants". She remembered being too tall for him and that wearing any kind of heel would make him upset, so she had looked for something appropriate and low. Her height was constantly commented upon in this country where the majority were of small stature. She thought how admired her height had been in Canada, how many friends in high school had envied her. She had been considered to be one of those people who had it all, looks, intelligence and élan. Here she felt uncomfortable, big and gauche. It took her a few passes to get used to the ritual greeting of the kiss on the cheek without moving to the wrong side of the face and causing awkward encounters that were intimate, where they were supposed to be gratuitous.

Emotional chaos racked the family even as the family hierarchy was at play the night they arrived in Mexico from the States, flying to return the body of this man to the country he had adopted as his home. She had sat for two and a half hours in silence in the cocoon of the small jet, uncomfortable to be part of the group without Nacho, he his mother's companion on another plane. Everyone had been wrapped in their own thoughts, tears shed silently, privately, even in that intimate space. The three private planes that had flown with the family landed in the humid subtropical night to crowds of hundreds waiting on the tarmac. The planes approached to land in the encroaching duskiness of departing sunlight. Flashing orange and yellow lights from police cars and landing lights had fractured the darkness, shooting their beams over the crowds of people. The warm, humid air had engulfed her when she picked her way gingerly down the small steps of the plane as hands reached up to help her; the jet engines continuing to whine behind her, the smell of the jet fuel mixed with that of the tropical vegetation. The flashing lights and the mass of bodies pressing in upon her were disorienting. "*Lo siento*" was murmured to her over and over, the embrace, the kiss of salutation a repeated ritual as they tried to get her through the crowds to the car. "*Ven para ca.*" Nacho's loss was supposed to be her loss, his family's loss, her loss too. It had felt so awkward to be a part of that moment. She hadn't belonged to his family and didn't belong there, but she wanted to support him. His priority had been to be supportive of his family, his blood. His commitment to her had been secondary, and someday, when they would have children, would be less than that. In his world, what counted was blood, not love or marriage. He couldn't help her adjust and fit in. She had to do it one step at a time, finding her way from one world to the next with her instincts and abilities to guide her. He couldn't be there to hold her hand and it didn't even occur to him that he should. His family needed him, and that was where he needed to be, wanted to be, with his blood.

Looking across the tarmac, she could see the shock suppressed as Nacho deplaned. He was stoic as he moved through the hundreds of grasping hands and gruff embraces, pushed through the throngs of people to her side. Together at last, they got into the back seat of a car, closing out the noise and pressing bodies. As the car broke slowly through the crowd, vehicles, police-cars, whining planes and flashing lights thinned behind them. They passed the hearse waiting for his father. It was surreal. She felt like a character in a movie. Her hand crept over the seat to cover his. He looked straight ahead. The friend in front looked over the seat at her and nodded in encouragement.

Was that was how the process of bereavement began, with documents and planes and a reception committee of hundreds of people? She couldn't understand how dealing with hundreds of people could help, and was still more bewildered when they arrived at a funeral parlour that looked like the lobby of an elegant hotel to be greeted by more engulfing crowds of people. The crowds were so thick that they had to fight to stay together as they pushed against them, one after another offering condolences, the ritual gesture of shaking hands, the quick embrace and a kiss to one cheek becoming an automatic sequence, repeated over and over again.

"El cuerpo esta aqui," they told them. They moved through the people to a dimly lit chapel on the far side of the room. It held no more than fifty people. The prayers began as they stood against the wall, a chanting, rhythmic repetition of human voices, murmuring in unison, began a ritual of mourning that was familiar to them, soothing to them, well rehearsed to them, but unfamiliar to her. A different culture than her own was teaching her the ritual they used to assuage the pain from the loss of a beloved and respected human being. This was how those who were left behind dealt with death. Ritual helped to numb the pain. There would be time to be alone and mourn their loss as a family, as sons and daughters, as a wife, but this was a community here to show their support and respect for this family and its dead patriarch, in unison.

Death gives meaning to life.

The prayers continued all the next day and into the evening. She had to stay on her feet most of the time because there were so many people there weren't enough chairs or even room to put them anywhere. The constant press of people continued unabated and the effort to understand what they were saying combined with the stress of being "on" for two days in a row without respite had worn her down. She stood near Nacho as the funeral mass proceeded. They were off to the side of the crowd, not with the rest of the family front and center in a room so packed full they couldn't move. Nacho was oblivious to her as he watched the ceremony. The smoke from the burning incense permeated the room. She didn't feel well. She leaned to the left as the room began to swim around her. She reached for his arm as she lost her balance. Startled, he grabbed her. "What's wrong with you? What are you doing?" "I'm sorry. I don't feel well" "Didn't you eat?" "I don't remember." "Why didn't you eat?" "I don't know. There wasn't time, I guess. I don't remember." The crowd parted to let them through. He took her outside to get some air. People looked at them curiously, the son and the foreign girlfriend, as they left the funeral service of his father. She was mortified as he waited for her to get her bearings in the muggy air. They missed the rest of the funeral service. By the time she felt well enough to go back in, it was over, the people beginning to pour out of the chapel into the night.

> **They are suddenly transported to a new land, where the beings around them know nothing of their history, and share none of their ideas — where their mother earth shows another lap, and human life has other forms than those on which their souls have been nourished.**

She knew as she looked at his image that this is what this powerful man had wanted for his son. It had been obvious from the beginning, that first time she met Nacho in Mexico, that if he could have arranged it and been able to control his son's choice of a spouse, that it would have been her. Greek girls were non-existent in Mexico. Pure, Greek girls of unmixed background that would strengthen the bloodlines and traditions were what he desired for his sons.

> **What man arranges, circumstances disarrange.**

But what none of them had fully understood was that her heritage was as much a part of where she had been raised as the blood that ran in her veins. She was an Anglo-Greek who had been a child in the sixties when Vancouver still strongly felt its ties to the British Commonwealth. They wanted a Greek without traditions different than their own.

The world she grew up in as a child was a world where the doors to the house didn't need to be locked, where she played safely and freely outside, where her baby sitter was Scottish, the green grocer at the corner English, where she sang "London Bridge is Falling Down" at school and sucked on Beech-Nut black licorice candies. She had played British Bulldog with the neighborhood children, in the rain, on lawns that were as thick and green as those in the British Isles and eaten Peak Frean cookies with tea and milk from glass bottles delivered to the door of the house. She had sung "God Save the Queen" and "Oh Canada" at school, even as Punch and Judy puppet shows played in Stanley Park. In Vancouver, cherry blossoms coated the trees in spring, the sound of foghorns echoed on cold fall mornings and the smell of the cool sea air blowing in pervaded the city. She had spoken both Greek and English all her life, eaten *"galactoboureko"* and hot dogs, played with her Greek cousins and her Canadian neighbours. She had been to the

United States, Greece and England by the time she was eleven, but the trip she took to Mexico at the age of fifteen changed her life forever.

When she went to Mexico that first time, it had been for a winter holiday at the newly developed resort of Mazatlan. Her parents had been excited to take them to a foreign country, and the palm trees, the warm sun, the beaches with the thatched palapas, the hotel lobby with bellhops in white guayaberas and mariachi music playing were all new experiences. They tried ceviche, tacos, huevos rancheros, refried beans and had gone to the local farmer's markets to experience an authentic part of the local culture. Everything had been so new and foreign, even though her Greek family felt a certain affinity with a culture where children were adored, family life respected, and an attitude that life was not meant to be taken too seriously, pervasive.

The musicians, the hops in the lobby, the tour guides that spoke English didn't live a reality shared by many Mexicans though. She had never seen such poverty. The dirt, the hunger, the disorder, the lack of social structure to address the overwhelming need shared by the majority of the people they saw outside of the hotel grounds, were a cultural shock.

Where there is hunger, law is not regarded; where law is not regarded, there will be hunger.

Nacho's sister, Aspacia, and her own older sister, Angela, had become friends a year before when his sister Aspacia had gone to Vancouver for a year to learn English. The pretty girl of Greek decent from Mexico had been a big hit that first day of school when the new boarders had introduced themselves at the Convent's morning assembly. She had spoken animatedly of her six brothers and sisters, her family's farming business and life in Culiacan. Aspacia and Angela had hit it off and become friends immediately, and Aspacia had been a frequent guest at her home all that year.

Now they were in Mazatlan, Mexico, three hours away from Aspacia's home, and she wanted to repay the hospitality shown her when she was in Canada. Angela, her mother, father and herself, had been invited to Culiacan to spend New Year's Eve with Aspacia's family; the Greeks from Canada and the Greek-Mexican family from Mexico were to get acquainted and ring in the New Year together.

Their Mexican hosts were a big family. As she had sat in the living room of their home that first night, children playing and running around, the adults talking to her parents, she hadn't felt a participant but an observer, a feeling enhanced as she had seen Aspacia talking to her twenty-one-year old brother, Nacho. It was obvious that they were talking about her as they sat across from her and Aspacia leant down to speak into his ear and pointed across to her feet in their flat, strappy sandals. She hadn't known if she was pointing out that her toenails weren't painted or that her sandals were flat, not high heeled, both unusual details in this country where every feminine accoutrement was used to enhance appearance, and every detail of appearance observed and commented upon. As the foreigners, she and her family noticed and commented upon how attractive the women in Aspacia's family were, beautiful even with the copious amounts of makeup they all wore and the elaborate hair do's. They had also noticed how the women, daughters and wives, had served the men their food after it had been put on the table for dinner that night.

> Women are sent out into the world as packages to be looked over or overlooked.

Hers was a family of four, theirs, at that time, a family of eighteen. She was reserved and read books as fast as she could get her hands on them; Aspacia was a character born to socialize, and it was doubtful if she had ever read a book. She had on mascara and lipgloss, Aspacia had painted her eyelids baby blue and wore so much mascara that her eyelids looked heavy and weighted down. The parents got along as though they had known each other all their lives, finding much common ground in their love and commitment to their families.

Nacho was the most reserved. He had looked at her thoughtfully as his sister chattered in his ear, gesturing towards her. She had heard stories about him from Aspacia over the last year, how he had gone to school in California, to Ojai, and how he had gone on to the University of Arizona. She had heard the stories of how he had crashed and trashed cars and motorcycles, one motorcycle accident leaving him in a coma for two days, how he was the wild one his parents couldn't control, how he was always by his father's side when his dad was around, how he did his own thing. He was the "American" brother, the one that liked to be in the States the best. She had looked at him, wondering what they were talking about. She had felt too young to be of any interest to him. Aspacia had often teased her about her quiet ways, playing the older sophisticate to her youth and inexperience.

"There's a dance at the country club tomorrow night for New Years that we are all going to, and since you don't speak Spanish, we thought it would be a good idea if Nacho kept you company. You brought a dress didn't you, because it's formal." "Yes, I did." "Good, then that's settled. Nacho will take care of you."

She had worried that he wouldn't be too happy to be stuck with a fifteen year old. He hadn't looked too happy, but it was out of her control. At the dinner, the family had milled around the living room with its marble floor, ornate furniture and carved wood paneling as she sat in her chair and waited to go back to the hotel. It was obvious that her parents and Angela were having a good time. She wanted to leave. She hadn't felt comfortable there. Nacho had got up and left his chair when Aspacia came over to talk to her. "What did you think of my brother?" "Oh, he seems nice," she had answered politely. She had found him rather good looking and thought of all the daring things he had done. Aspacia chatted on about the dance tomorrow and how many people would be there— all of Culiacan it seemed, and how her family would get a big table and sit together. At fifteen, she had been excited about the New Years dance, not yet old enough to be bored with that sort of event, and happy for any opportunity to dress up.

The next night, someone had come to the hotel to pick them up and take them up to the family home. She had walked into their marble floored foyer, her wide skirt swinging over her feet in flat, patent sandals. Her dress was made of layers of brown gauze patterned with little pink roses. It belled out from a wide waistband and two wide bands of fabric came up from the waist, covering her breasts and tying at the neck in a filmy bow that trailed behind her to the ground. She had felt pretty and loved the dress she was wearing. Nacho, in a tuxedo, and an older sister of his, pregnant, in a long dress, came out of the kitchen. They talked animatedly as they approached her. It didn't look like a pleasant discussion. Without speaking to her, Nacho's sister took her arm, pulled her over and tugged Nacho with her other hand. She turned them so that they were facing apart and back-to-back. With or without language it was clear that he was not going to accompany her if she didn't pass the height test. She was so glad that she was wearing flats. She was so embarrassed. They ignored her and continued to talk, then Nacho left for another part of the house. "Is everything all right? He doesn't have to go with me if he doesn't want to. He must have his own friends he wants to be with." "Oh no, that's all right. He just wanted to make sure that you weren't going to be taller than him when you danced."

When they arrived at the country club, it had been full of elegantly dressed people. Almost everyone in the family spoke English, and the two fathers happily conversed all night in Greek. The conversation was lively around the long table as dinner was served by the black-coated waiters. After dinner, Nacho and she had turned their chairs so that they could more easily talk to one another.

"You look very pretty," he'd said. Then he had reached over and touched the hair that waved below her ear. "You should let your hair grow long," he said, "It would look better on you than short hair."

"I had hair down to my waist until a couple of months ago. I wanted a change and I cut it." She hadn't known how to take the backhanded compliment. It had seemed rude to her, that he would tell her to change her hair at the same time that he told her she looked nice. She hadn't felt like she looked nice anymore. "Would you like to dance?" he asked. "Yes, sure," she replied. They stood and moved to the packed dance floor. She could see all four parents looking at them with approval as he held her and started to move to the rhythm of the music. This was a different beat than anything she had heard before. It was very fast, loud and trumpety, with bassoons and rattling drums in the tune. He held her very close, so close her cheek and body were pressed tightly against his. His feet moved quickly, in small steps, as he whirled her around, her dress belling out behind her. It worked well for this type of dance that they were the same height. She had never danced like this before. She loved to move to the rhythm of music and loved to dance on her own all the time. This was different. It was so close and tight it was uncomfortably intimate. She had to let her body relax completely and let him control the direction they would go in, like a puppet, in order to follow him. But to be that close to an attractive, older boy whom she had only known for a day was not conducive to relaxation. She kept misstepping and treading on his feet, throwing them both off. She kept apologizing as they would stop and start over again, trying to regain the rhythm of the music. She wanted them to play "Chicago," anything American, so that she could show that she really could dance, that she wasn't a total klutz.

Finally the song had ended and they went to sit down, both excited by their close contact and tired from the effort of trying to dance in unison. Both sets of parents smiled from across the table, but Nacho's father was beaming.

The next day they went to the family house in the afternoon, everyone tired from their late night out. When they arrived, the married sisters with their husbands and children stood outside the tall, stone wall that encompassed the perimeter of the house. The iron-gate and its lock were open as family members went in and out. She sat on the lower portion of the wall and watched the lively group engaged in conversation as plans were made for their excursion that day. She saw a little raggedy boy move towards the group from across the street. He carried a bucket in his hand filled with shoe polish and brushes. He was dark brown with dirt in his coarse, black hair, thin and barefoot, wearing a tattered, dirty shirt and pants. He looked no more than six years old. He approached Nacho's father and talked to him. The old man called to his little grandson— blonde, brown-eyed and wearing a striped cotton shirt, khaki pants and brown shoes. She had noticed the little boy was his favorite grandson, often carried about and indulgently treated. The child was settled on the wall next to her. The little boy sat patiently as the other, almost of identical stature, brushed and cleaned his shoes for him. She watched and saw that no one else saw anything out of the ordinary, they saw nothing incongruous in one child serving another. Finally, the shoes were polished and the little dark "*boleador*" was sent on his way with a couple of pesos more than he had asked for in his hand from Nacho's father.

She had known this man, this patriarch, mainly through observation. They hadn't had a conversation in the five years she'd known the family before he died, and yet, the images she had of him were as clear and vivid as the last one she had of him in his casket. As she put the frame back down on the bureau amongst the other family members, she saw their images joined together in the gleam of the smooth lacquer. Greek, Mexican, new generations and old, all were joined together in the reflective surface that collected their families. They had created one family from two and woven them together in a bridged culture that allowed their diversity to cross over to a new world that blended traditions and customs into one family and one blood that was uniquely their own. She looked at the black-and-white image of him one last time before she walked out of the room, the images of him taken with her as she went, his legacy, his blood, carried on in her children.

In order to survive, humans must provide for their material, emotional and intellectual needs. These are satisfied by culture, a complex system that includes tools, language and beliefs.

Chapter THREE

THE RING

She walked across the bathroom, over the cool limestone tiles to her vanity, and pulled open the beveled mirror front of the dark wood drawer. Her hand was reflected in the surface, one hand real, one an illusion— an image of a hand. Lined with scented, floral paper, the interior of the drawer glittered with stones and gold from the jewelry collected there. One heavy gold ring embossed with leaves and berries rested on top, distinct from the other pieces with its simple, large, center-set diamond. She picked it up and turned it over in her fingers, the fingers that would never wear it again. The design, her design, had a wide, hammered-gold background with polished bas-relief gold work on the band of simple laurel leaves and granulation. It was both classical and modern, the best of both eras, to her mind, reflecting both her heritage and her contemporary and pragmatic approach to design.

When Nacho had given her the stone, it had been set in a simple, yellow gold band. It had protruded above the surface of her hand in an obvious statement of proprietorship.

> **Visual signs of authority… the family device of the diamond ring,… the preeminent symbol of marital alliance**

The ring designated her as belonging to Nacho, his bride-to-be, his girl, his woman. He had not given it to her for months after they had made an undeclared commitment to one another. She had read enough romance novels and had been enough of a romantic at the age of twenty to hope that the occasion when some one asked her to be his bride would be somewhat special. Her destiny had been to be sitting in a car, at an intersection in Osoyoos, on a hot summer day in July, Nacho driving, when he had casually said to her, "Would you like to live in Nogales?" She had quickly tried to digest the import of his statement before she replied, "Yes." He had considered the deed done after that, and she had understood from his behaviour that that was it, that he wanted her to move there as his wife. They had passed a happy week together before he returned to the States; she had been too shy to ask him when anything more formal would be said to her family.

She had tickets paid to go to the American College in Athens, Greece for a year, her money in the bank there and her departure planned for the end of August, when Nacho, before departing for Nogales, said "You're not still going to Greece are you?" "Of course I am," she replied. "We won't be getting married until June anyway, and I'm supposed to leave in two weeks. Everything is ready." "I don't think you should go. We won't see each other. Why don't you cancel your plans and go to U.B.C. instead so that we can see each other during the year?" "My parents are going to be suspicious. I have to tell them something." "No you don't. Just tell them that you changed your mind." She had hoped this would have been the impetus for him to say something to her family, but he had left for the States without claiming her, as his own, to the people she wanted to share her happiness with, leaving her feeling uncomfortable and secretive, when her relationship with her parents had always been open and honest.

He had returned in October, overtly on a business trip, but they both knew it was to tell her parents that they planned to marry. Days passed, yet he didn't talk to her father. By the fifth day he called in backup. His older sister and her husband being nearby on a trip, he asked them to come to Vancouver to keep him company. They were suspicious; her mother was suspicious, but her father was determinately oblivious. Nacho's sister and brother-in-law had been in Vancouver for four days when they said that, while it had been nice to visit, it was time for them to be moving on. Nacho was under pressure to say something that night, before his support system left him.

They had all been at her home, sitting in the family room talking, when her father invited Nacho up to look at his shoes. He had often been shoeless growing up, his bare feet covered with paint in the few family pictures that were mementos of his childhood, so his collection of Bally shoes were his pride and joy, and he loved to show people he felt comfortable with the boxes of fine leather shoes wrapped in tissue. She, Nacho and her father had gone up together. She nudged Nacho. This was the moment to say something. Nacho had nudged her back, gesturing that it was for her to say. When her father had emerged from the closet carrying a stack of shoe boxes, she had said, "Daddy, there's something Nacho wanted to talk to you about." Nacho had looked acutely uncomfortable as her father absent mindedly replied, "What's that?" Taking his cue, Nacho opened with, "Actually we both wanted to say that, well, we thought that we would like to get married." "What, what did you say?" "Daddy, Nacho said that we want to get married." "Married! Why would you want to get married? You're too young, and your mom and I would be alone. You haven't finished school yet." "Well, we know that, Daddy, but we want to get married anyway." "I don't think that's a good idea. You have to wait. You aren't ready for marriage." "Well, maybe we are." "No, no you're not, and anyway, even if you were, you can't get married for at least a couple of years." "A couple of years! Daddy, we want to get married in June." "June! There's no way you can get married in June. It's out of the question." "But we are."

Think then that duty shall have dread to speak?

Her father had been so disappointed. This was not what she had envisioned at all, and Nacho looked unhappy as well. No one seemed pleased, considering they had just announced their "joyful" plans to marry. Her father had put away the shoe boxes and walked out of the room and down the semi-circular stairway without another word, then passed by her mother in the kitchen, Nacho and her trailing behind him. Her mother had known, of course, and had been waiting for the news to come downstairs, but nobody had known how to handle her father's sadness. Nacho's sister and brother-in-law had been expecting some sort of announcement, but were taken aback by her father's dour face. They had been uncomfortable asking what was going on. Nacho, she and her mother trickled in to the room and eventually, with a deep sigh, her father had said, "Well, it looks like Nacho and Tina are planning to get married." He may as well have said that they were planning to jump off a cliff. Somehow, congratulations didn't seem in order, but they were the appropriate thing to do in the circumstances, so her mother hugged them each in turn, as did his family, and they had taken out some wine to toast the occasion in a muted moment of supposed celebration.

Nacho's family had left and he had stayed on another week. She kept hoping that any day now he would give her a ring, but the days passed with no ring produced. Her relatives had an engagement party in their honour, and, of course, every one had asked to look at her hand, which was ringless. She had made up facile excuses as to why she had no ring as of yet, but she had felt sad, hurt and bewildered that he hadn't made an effort to buy her one, when she knew he could afford it.

The months had passed and her studies had suffered, as she had no interest in school anymore, only living for the time when she could be with Nacho everyday. The Christmas holidays came around and she flew down to Arizona, where he met her at the airport with his sister. Two days later they flew to Mexico to celebrate Christmas with all of his family in Culiacan. Christmas Eve in his family was such a different affair than in her own home, where there were just two children, as opposed to his family with seven siblings and dozens of nieces and nephews. Her parents had come down too, and Angela was now living in Mexico with her husband and little girl. Everyone was together—one big happy family. As was their tradition, the gifts were handed out as the midnight hour passed and the twenty-fifth began. Everyone in the family got multiple gifts and it was a time of happy chaos as names were called out, wrappings discarded and gifts shown off. Her name was called out and a medium-sized box handed to her. Everyone in the room quieted down and turned to watch her peel the brightly coloured wrapping from the box. She opened the box and nothing was inside but another box that was wrapped up; she opened that one too, only to find a third. By now everyone was calling out comments, laughing and waiting with anticipation to see her find the gift which she and they knew would be her ring. Her mind moved quickly to consider how everyone would be gauging her reaction to the ring. She had so wished that this would be a private moment and felt flustered and pressured as she came to yet another wrapped box. That had been the last one; a black velvet ring box was revealed, the single, large stone on its slim, gold band glittering in the light as she passed it around the room for all to see. It had definitely been a family event, as the ring finally came back to her only after all had seen it, then she put it on herself. Nacho had been pleased to share this special moment with their families. She had not.

> Defining gendered power and submission through the metaphor of marriage... the diamond ring became a gendered "symbol of rule,"... lending an appearance of legitimacy to a fundamentally illegitimate form of authority... creating an ideal image of consent."

Months later, playing with the ring, as was her habit, rubbing the edge of the stone with her nail, she had felt a ridge in the edge of the stone. "Nacho, the stone is cracked," she had told him. "It can't be, diamonds don't crack." "But this one is." He had taken it to his brother-in-law the jeweler, who sent it to have the stone exchanged for one of the caliber he paid for, and the ring had come back without a ridge. They discovered years later that the stone had been reset so that the flaw was occluded from view by the prong. The jeweler had never changed the stone, but had cheated them and returned the same diamond.

The slim, narrow band with the protruding stone had never been comfortable on her hand. The top-heavy setting kept the stone swinging on its side and the prongs caught on her clothes. She redesigned the ring, making it wide enough to sit on her finger comfortably. She had set the diamond in a bezel so that both the stone and her clothes would be protected. The laurel leaves were classical motifs from antiquity, as were the berries, and she had chosen them for the band because they represented success, loyalty and fruitful endeavor. They were the symbols she chose to represent her marital union, creating her own metaphor in gold and carbon for what she wanted in her marriage.

Nacho had worn his ring, a fairly simple gold band, for the duration of the honeymoon, then put it away, saying it was uncomfortable and that it was dangerous to wear when he was in the packing-house, where the wires on the boxes could catch it and hurt his hand. They had argued over it intermittently through the years, because he never chose to wear it, even when he wasn't working. Eventually the story had evolved that he had lost it, which she had believed until she found it in the bank's safety box a month after they had decided to divorce. She had designed him a signet ring with the crest she had made into his medallion when they married, and he had worn that one because, she imagined, it didn't look as matrimonial. Even now, as she looked at the ring in her bare hand that she felt no desire to adorn with a mark of possession, she felt resentful, angry, profoundly hurt, that she had been gullible enough to wear hers in good faith, while he abused that trust.

The hard stone exemplified the adamantine fidelity of its wearer.

The diamond glittered brightly in the vanity light. She found it ironic that he should still wear his now; now that his marriage was dissolving, he wore it everyday. Perhaps he had finally understood, to some degree, the notion that the ring on the ring finger controlled the heart of the wearer, the thin vein there proceeding directly to the heart. There was some justice to be found in the fact that he still wore his, while she did not.

And felt how awful goodness is, and saw virtue in her shape how lovely, saw and pin'ed his loss.

Her ring formed a perfect circle of gold, the craftsmanship and the goldsmithing exquisite and impeccable, the flaw in the diamond hidden from view. But it had been fate that the stone had been meant to be hers. The symbolism of the eternal circle of love had its own allegory in the circle of gold, in the hard, clear stone; all pure intent, ironically betrayed. The stone's true nature was flawed, just as the promises made to her had been. The ring that should have meant so much to her had sadly come to symbolize her compromised dreams, rather than the fruition of a loving and sustaining love.

She turned the ring over in her hand, still able to appreciate the beauty of it without any need for possession. She wouldn't wear it again. It had lost its ability to persuade her with the promise of possibility. Laying it in the drawer, she knew it didn't belong on her hand anymore.

As a sign, in the ceremony of the Holy Church, the husband places on the finger of his wife, a ring which is called faith. Whereby it is intended that the faith, or the ring of that faith, is a bond, in order to let you know that it is not permitted to you, man, to have another wife, while your first one is alive; and it is not permitted to you to have another wife or concubine... Moreover, note that the ring, called faith, is placed on the finger that is next to the little finger, where there is a vein which has its root in the heart; that is so as to let you know that you, who are in matrimony, ought to live cordially, and by loving cordially you ought to content each other without searching for another person.

Chapter FOUR

the bathing suit

She opened the door and walked into her dark closet as she flipped the light switch. Racks of clothes and shoes, belts and purses surrounded her with their presence, each one meant for a purpose, an occasion. They were also a reflection of who she was to a world that judged her by how she looked and what she wore. In the back of the closet, closed away in a cardboard hat-box, were her bathing suits. She had enjoyed wearing bathing suits; they reminded her of her parent's place in the Okanogan, in Canada, where she had spent every summer of her life, spending every day at the beach, "brown as a little Indian," as her mother had said, from day after day in the sun. In a bathing suit, at the lake, she had been her most happy and free self, diving and swimming for hour after hour, from morning till night, just another creature at home outside, in the fresh air, in the water, in the sun.

The lake where she had played for many happy years was nestled at the bottom of the surrounding blue-grey mountains, ringed by lush orchards doubled over by the apples, pears, plums and peaches that they carried every summer. The town of Osoyoos held a few hundred people that lived in a charming, clean and quiet little village full of gardens, pretty green lawns and bursting flower beds. Flowers and tall shade trees filled the front yards and vegetable gardens grew among the fruit trees in the back. People walked to the ice cream parlour, to the barber's and to the local beaches, where they lay on the grass, lazing in the summer sun.

In the summer the town was inundated with visitors. Youthful vagrants from Quebec came to find summer employment in the orchards and visitors from Vancouver and Alberta came for the bright sun, fresh fruits and warm weather of the only pocket desert in Canada. The town was so pretty and charming it was the pride and joy of its citizens, ranking, "second most beautiful town in the world" to a village in Scotland.

As she pulled out her practical black suit, another one, bright and flowery, fell out of the box. She picked it up and remembered the last time she had worn it, the summer her second son had been born and they had gone to the Okanogan as a family, with her two- year old and her husband, to spend a couple of weeks at the lake with her parents. Her mum and dad and Nacho hadn't wanted her to miss the annual holiday at the beach, so they had come with their newborn and small son to enjoy the sand, the lake and the support of family as they adjusted to their new addition.

She loved the lake. She had spent every summer on its shores since the age of six and was happiest at the beach, in a swimsuit, tanning and swimming the day away as ski boats and skiers droned by offshore. There was a new drone this year, the drone of the engine caused by the "ultralight," set up by a new opportunist down the beach. They watched the brightly coloured wings fly up and over the lower slopes of the mountain, time after time, all day long, gliding to a splash down in the water in front of her family's hotel.

It looked like great fun and they imagined what the view of the lake and the valley would look like from a bird's eye view. She loved to do that which was different and daring, even though Nacho tended to worry about worst case scenarios. Being at the beach wasn't the same with him as in years past. Now there was his constant vigilance of her slim body in her swimsuit as he anticipated the glances thrown her way by other men around them. The birth of her second son hadn't changed her figure at all, which, as far as he was concerned, was both a good and a bad thing.

> **The body is that portion of nature with which each moment of human experience ultimately co-operates.**

Looking after her two small boys and trying to please Nacho by wearing a T-shirt over her suit, she watched the small plane day after day and thought what fun it would be to try a new adventure, how nice it would feel to be as light as air with the wind rushing past, the sun above and the lake below. "Please. It would be such fun. Why don't we try it? Look how many people have gone and nothing bad has happened." "What if something does happen though? We have two sons to look after. This isn't the time to be foolish." "Oh don't be so negative. Nothing bad is going to happen. If you're worried about me, you go first and I'll watch," she joked.

Her mum and dad offered to sit on the beach with the baby and their little son as they walked along the shore, through the floats, paddle boats, splashing children, beach chairs and umbrellas to the gay kiosk the aviator had set up on the sand. "How much does it cost and how long will it take?" Nacho asked the pilot. "The ride takes about twenty five minutes each and if you're both going, I'll give you a special price," he said as he glanced past Nacho to her. Arrangements were made and Nacho strapped himself in, while she stood in the water and watched. The plane was an assembly of aluminum tubes, wire cables and brightly coloured canvas. The seats were black nylon slings, barely big enough to hold a person, but amply rigged with straps and buckles to ensure the passengers didn't fall out of their motorized kite. The canvas and aluminum contraption droned across the water and soon became airborne, buzzing above her, diminishing in size as it rose higher and higher. She wondered how cool it was with the air speed and lack of protection offered by the frame of the plane. She was glad she had put shorts and a T-shirt over her suit, ready for when her turn came. The plane returned from its rise over the lower hills at the bottom of the mountain and began its descent to the lake. When it was directly overhead, as the pilot had said he would do, he turned off the engine to glide down to the water, using the force of the air and the flaps and paddles to control its descent. It glided down in a perfect swoosh of air and splashing water to the shore where she waited.

"Was it fun?" she asked. "It was great," he replied. "Really nice. You're going to like it." He got out of his seat so that she could get in, and the pilot helped her adjust her straps and buckles. As the metal and canvas contraption taxied over the smooth water and began to rise over the lake, she could imagine her two-year-old, Thano, on the beach, craning his head to watch, and Nacho, far below, watching her ascent. The lakeshore was covered with confetti-like coloured spots as the plane buzzed higher and higher. They were higher than Nacho had gone; they were higher than she had ever seen the little kite go over the past few days. "How long are you here for?" the pilot asked her. "Another week," she replied and added, "We sure seem to be very high." "Yeah, you look adventurous. I thought that you might enjoy the higher view. So what are you doing tonight?" "Pardon me?" "Well, I just thought that you might like to go out tonight." "I'm married," she said. "I didn't ask you if you were married," he replied and reached over and shut off the engine. "What are you doing?" she said calmly enough, but they both knew that she was scared. All she could hear was the sound of the air rushing through the metal and canvas frame. The wind turned them towards the mountain and she guessed that they were too high to glide down. "I thought that you looked adventurous. If you don't like it, you turn it on and fly. It's not hard. You saw me do it. So would you like to go out tonight?" "This isn't funny." She tried to sound calm, but his cocky attitude and the nonchalant manner in which he played with the flaps and pedals, turning the plane back and forth in the wind, was terrifying. He grinned at her "Are you scared?" he taunted her. "All you have to do is say you'll go out with me and I'll turn the engine on." "Look, I'm married," she said. "I didn't ask you if you were married." She didn't think that he would risk his life for a night out with her, but he may have made a mistake in assuming that the engine would turn on when he wanted it to. "Look, I have a six-week old baby down on the beach. Would you please turn on the engine?" "I didn't ask you if you had a baby. I asked you if you want to go out tonight." She thought of how she wished she looked like she had had a baby six weeks ago, so that this wouldn't be happening to her. "Look mister, my husband and my father are both going to be very unhappy with you if you don't turn on the engine." "You think that I care what your husband and your father will do? Lady, we are very far up here. I'm the one in control, not you, or your husband, or your father." She tried a new approach as the plane moved farther away from the shore and the mountain. Now, they floated over the center of the lake, so far up she couldn't make out anything below except splashes of colour. A seagull flew next to them, catching a ride from the plane's current. "Look, you seem like a very nice guy, and you have a great business, what do you want with a married woman like me?" She smiled as she finished.

He looked at her and laughed. "So you'll go out?" "Sure," she said. "It would be fun. You look like a guy that knows how to have a good time." He snickered. He knew that she had to give in. They both knew. That was what he wanted. He leaned over and turned the engine on. Further conversation was difficult over the noise and she just wanted to start breathing again as he turned the plane and began to descend.

> **A concern for one's own safety in the face of dangers real and immediate was the process of a rational mind.**

The plane glided down and she saw Nacho standing on shore waiting. They dropped down and hit the water, the splash wetting her and the pilot both. They bumped over the waves towards the gay tourists on their bright floats. As they got closer to Nacho, she thought of the fist-fight he had had at a club when some guy had asked her to dance, unnoticeably pregnant at six months. She thought of the argument they'd had after she had talked too long to a friend of his. She remembered the friends, her university buddies, whom she hadn't invited to their wedding to avoid a fight. She thought of how he was always telling her to fix her clothes, cover up, even if she thought she looked fine. "You were gone a long time. Your ride took over thirty minutes. Why did you take so long?" He looked annoyed and suspicious. "Oh, was it that long? Wow, I didn't notice." "And you went up much higher than I did too." "Yeah, I did, it was really interesting to go up that high." The pilot stood beside his motorized kite and watched them. He knew that she wasn't going to say anything. "Nacho, you don't mind if I run off do you? I feel badly that I've left my mum with the kids so long." "No, go ahead. You have been gone too long." She didn't look back as she walked quickly down the beach.

She put the swimsuits back in the box, thinking of that day, how all of her life, except for a few years between the age of six and thirteen, she had attracted an unsolicited amount of attention by her appearance. It had affected her in so many ways, one of them being to develop a very thin skin in regards to the way people are judged solely according to appearance, which as a Greek was a given. Greeks pour over the fashion collections every season, and even in her mother's small village in central Greece they know who Dolce and Gabbana and Gucci were, because it is part of their culture to know and follow the current fashions. It was also part of their culture to appreciate while being immune to physical beauty, having set the standard for much of western civilization with their art. Having a nice physique made it worse. Pretty and plump was tolerable; pretty tall and nicely dressed created a walking target.

Never judge from appearance.

Catcalls on the street, notes from waiters, group phone calls from guys dorms, men old enough to be her father or grandfather asking her out to dinner, to a bar, celebrities, men at adjoining tables sending waiters to get her number, a gay classmate from high school hitting on her, guys not asking her out because they were afraid she would be conceited, and the mistress of studies in grade eleven telling her after her grades dropped from A's to A's and B's, "you're not going to get through life on your looks."

Society assumes that looking good equals power.

A guy at a party convincing someone to hit the light switch so that he could grab her in the dark, another guy refusing to give directions unless she ponied up a kiss, a young man walking up to her in a store and saying that she was the most beautiful woman he had ever seen and another man driving by while she was putting her groceries in the car, calling out, "You made my day." A good friend's father trying to kiss her on the mouth as he helped her put her small boys in the car, her husband's cousin pursuing her with his eyes for hours on end and, as the years passed, her teenage sons' rival telling him, "Your mom is hot." There was her parent's pride in her appearance, her sister's envy, her husband's fear and her own discomfort, pleasure and resentment.

She had been reading the same list to her therapist of over two years, finally comfortable enough to be open with him when he interjected, "And as the British would say, your therapist wants to get in your knickers." She had been shocked, unable to decide from his deadpan face, whether he had really said it or not. He had continued writing on his notepad as though he had said the most ordinary thing in the world. Nobody had ever said anything so blatant to her. This man, this man she believed to have the highest integrity, who had helped her believe in herself, related to her on the same level all the other men did who had treated her as a piece of meat. What was wrong that even someone who had come to know her so intimately, couldn't get past the exterior, expressing a desire to get in her "knickers?"

These hidden beauties are commonly by far the greatest, because the more complex a beauty is, the more hidden is it.

Nacho had never enjoyed taking her out. He had developed eyes in the back of his head to see if anyone was watching her and yet seemed oblivious to the obvious ones, like his cousin, or the therapist, who made moves that divulged their baser intentions with impunity. She had cut off contact with all of her male friends after they married. He preferred her home, unless he was with her or unless she was with girlfriends, or family. She learned that any infractions of his rules brought on a fight, so, sometimes she did, sometimes she avoided it. She became very sensitive to any situation that would provoke him, learning to defend herself more ably than she had that day on the beach rather than depend on him and cause herself more grief.

She would always be grateful that her parents had made her healthy and whole. It had been her fate, and her fate gave her a sensitivity that she might not otherwise have had. It also made her more defensive of those that were discriminated against because of their skin colour, race, religion, appearance or gender. There were too many people who were marginalized members of society, and being one of a victimized group of any kind, she learned to identify with the fact that how people felt was the most important aspect of themselves as human beings, in spite of the massive amounts of attention given to appearance.

To look... is very different from seeing... One does not see until one sees its beauty. Then and then only, does it come into existence.

Chapter FIVE

The Candlesticks

Passing between the cast-iron balusters framing the tall double doorway, she climbed up the stone stairs to the family room. To her right, two oversized velvet chairs flanked the flickering fire, the one on the left, her chair, the chair on the right, Nacho's. She sat down, let her slippers fall onto the warm cream and brown wool of the Persian carpet and propped her feet on the footstool with its silky, leopard fabric. The fireplace mantle was supported by the half-naked figures of two young boys, peeling gesso and soot from fires past giving a mottled patina to their forms. With its cast-iron whorls and arabesques, the fireplace grate cast an elegant silhouette against the endless patterns of the flickering flames. It was an inviting nook in the big room, weighted by time past in its heavy oak beams, framed fossils and antique castle engravings.

Between the two chairs stood a tray table, hand-painted with the figures of two golden lions facing one another in angry confrontation, their ferocious faces signaling perpetual conflict. To one side of the lions were a pair of candlestick holders carved from wood into a pair of feet wearing simple sandals. They were the feet and sandals of a simple man, a peon, a peon's feet next to the regal cats. The lions seemed to follow her marriage's history, the united lion's with one head on the mantlepiece, the beginning, the separate and confrontational lions, what their marriage was now. The feet in their simple footwear harkened back to her's and Nacho's family history. She had imagined when she found them that they were not unlike the sandals her father or her father-in-law would have worn in Greece as poor young farmers, and not unlike the feet she saw shod similarly today in the tomato fields, on the farms in Culiacan. The workers toiled up and down the long rows of plants in the hot sun, the sun-scorched soil heating feet through flimsy footwear.

As she lit the candles, she savoured the scent of the burning wick and melting beeswax. She thought of her favorite feet, her children's feet, of how she had nibbled and caressed them when they were small, those pudgy, infant feet, with rosy toes and tender new skin, the most perfect symbol of dependency and innocence. Those feet now, barefoot and relaxed, resting on an ottoman as they watched television in this room, filled her with love and gratitude that they had grown up to be strong and healthy, able to carry her grown-up children where they needed to go. She remembered how one of her favorite things about being a couple had been to find another pair of feet to twine with hers under the covers, in bed, the contact reassuring her that she was not alone. She thought of how her favorite footwear, in spite of the shelves of designer shoes in her closet, were a pair of gym socks or slippers worn around the house, comfortable and clean, cozy and grounding.

She had chosen the flooring of the house because of the way the Portuguese limestone felt cool and smoothly soapy under her bare feet. In this warm climate, where the sun readily warmed any surface exposed to its burning heat, this home with its high ceilings and cool, light stone floors effectively and subtly deflected the fierceness of the climate, grounding the house and giving it much of its disposition.

She had read that feet represented stability, freedom and enlightenment when used in works of art. So many good things in such a simple symbol. As the appendage that allowed mobility and freedom to move about and know the world, they were the primary source the body used to draw energy from the earth into the body. She thought of the many valiant people she saw every day in wheelchairs and of how, despite their handicaps, they impressed her with their determination to live a full life without the mobility most were privileged to have and without the contact with earth and soil to connect them to their world.

The journey of a thousand miles starts from beneath your feet.

She thought of the gift it was to feel the sand between her toes, gravel cut into her soles, and to feel the warmth of a pair of feet next to hers. What it was like to feel the burning heat of a hot sidewalk, cool, springy grass, tight shoes and soft slippers. To run, to dance, to walk, to kick, to jiggle, to stand on tippy toe, to stride, to jive, to skate, to jump, to caress. Feet were the way in which humans first strove for independence and autonomy. She recalled her children's first tottering steps away from her when they learned to walk and how they would howl with indignation when she caught them and carried them back to where they had begun. Every human's journey was one to self sufficiency and independence, the ubiquitous journey inevitable to all. Children begin by walking, following their instincts at a young age, and know it is unnatural to go back. A journey to self knowledge should move forward, as the feet did.

My feet are thrust forward when I desire to walk.

She remembered seeing a program on television showing a young man conceived in the thalidomide era demonstrating how he fed himself, groomed himself and played the drums with his impeccably clean and useful feet, all because he was born without arms. For him they were doubly blessed because they were his independence in ways most people could never imagine. Her own feet let her express her joy in an impromptu dance, a run to keep her heart in good health, gifting her with the mobility to go wherever she wanted. She always parked far away from where she needed to go because of the pleasure she found in walking. She was fortunate that her feet were strong and that she could walk for miles and not tire. She enjoyed it, and the word "joy" truly expressed the feelings of autonomy and self sufficiency her two feet gave her.

> The path may be rocky and twisted, but the world is waiting for that special contribution each of us was born to make.

She had found that feet and footwear said so much about the people they belonged to. Age, class, economics, gender, lifestyle, grooming and taste were all fairly well represented in their choices. Long toenails, chipped nail polish, clean nails, dirty nails, calloused feet, dry skin, dirty boots, polished oxfords, high heels, ratty sneakers, rubber flip flops, pink booties, mini blue socks, slim feet, stocky feet, soft brown-tanned skin, pale, dry, cracked skin. Living where the weather was warm and where people's feet were often exposed created a parade of humanity that never failed to intrigue her.

Nacho had slim feet for a man, slim and flat. A scar was visible on his right foot, above the ankle, where he had had a steel plate inserted to help the shattered bone heal. He had broken it falling down the stairs outside this room when he had tried to carry her to the car, to take her to the hospital. He had slipped on the last stair and, to save her from crashing onto the stone floor, had borne both their weights on his leg, fracturing the bone in three places. And all because she had innocently taken a capful of cough medicine that morning, not realizing that she was allergic to the medication. Anaphylactic shock had soon set in and Nacho had tried to carry her to the car, and fallen. She remembered lying on the stone floor, far enough away from him that she couldn't touch him, and looking over to see the bone sticking out of his flesh. She had been so weakened she had hardly been able to say, "Nacho, your leg is broken." He had called for help and eventually two ambulances had come to take them to the hospital.

He had suffered terribly as a boy when he had broken his left leg, then broken it again, at last having it rebroken by the doctors to reset it. Now he had broken his right leg because of her. The shock of their fall and seeing his injured leg had set her own adrenaline rushing and counteracted the toxic affect of the medication. The accident had saved her life, the doctors told them as they were both treated in the emergency room at the hospital. Saved her life, but weakened his leg forever. The doctors told him not to run on it ever again. She always felt guilty when the weather was damp and it bothered him. The accident had happened ten years ago, the year they moved into the house. None of their families had lived nearby, the closest ones being in Culiacan. As he had been recovering in the hospital in Nogales, his mother and Angela had flown in to be with him in his surgery when the doctors set the bones together.

It was a story that grew thin as they repeated it over the years. "What a story. What a man," people would say and rib him. They didn't know how much it bothered him, but she did. She remembered his anger and frustration, his simmering temper as he dealt with the inconvenience and pain of the healing process. He had never blamed her, but she was the only one who really knew how much he had been affected by that incident. He had, however, played the role others expected of him very well, being deprecating, dismissive, nonchalant and tough. Anything rather than show what he really felt.

She thought of the strongest feet she knew, those of her father. They were broad feet, strongly formed, with high arches and well-formed toes. He often recounted tales of his experience in the mountains of Greece as a sixteen-year-old soldier, how he had walked hundreds of miles with his troops, covered in lice, without food or water for days, often barefoot as he hid and fought in the mountains to free his country. His foot too had a scar above the ankle on his right foot. He was seventy-seven now and his leg had never healed quite as it had been before his accident two years ago.

He had been up in the hills above Osoyoos, hunting alone, as he often did in the Fall. He was a man passionately in love with the outdoors, as were many hunters. He never felt afraid to go alone in the forests as he looked for game. That day, he had left his Jeep and walked into the forest some distance from his car when he saw a large buck. He had excitedly loaded his gun, and in his excitement, not looked where he was stepping. His right foot had plunged into a rabbit hole, snapping his leg in two just as the gun misfired next to his head. It had taken him three hours to drag himself through the undergrowth to his car, his leg unstabilized, flopping back and forth like a rag doll's. He had had a hard time getting into the car, as it was his right leg, but he had succeeded at last and driven to the highway, where he could finally call for help. R.C.M.P. had taken him to the hospital, where her mother and Angela waited anxiously as they pieced the fragments of bone together with a steel plate.

She thought how ironic it was that both her father and her husband had broken the same leg in such unique circumstances, musing over how they were both changed by their experience and loss of autonomy. Their women, her mother and herself, had been the caretakers, and had helped them heal in a long recovery process. So many people had been affected by their accidents. Spouses, children, employees, but most of all, they themselves had been changed. Both of them now had a weakness. For both men it had changed their perception of themselves, of who they were and where they were safe. For her father, it had been a traumatic experience akin to what he had experienced in the war, once more with no one and nothing to save him except himself. For Nacho, breaking his leg had been an unwelcome reminder of a childhood trauma that had deprived him of freedom for months and had created a dependence and a weakness he abhorred. Her father had often thanked whatever luck had saved his leg, allowing it to be used again to take the walks and swims he so enjoyed. For Nacho, his weakened leg was a bitter thorn in his side, one more debility.

Beneath appearance, an inner reality.

She and her mother spent months taking care of their husbands in their progress toward recovery. She had been witness to Nacho's process more than her father's, and her perception of him had been changed, as well as his of himself. She had often unfairly compared his situation to others more dire and been less than compassionate. But she had, ultimately, not had anyone to look after her when she needed someone to look after her most. Her accident had been traumatic as well, and she had felt very alone and uncared for as his family and well wishers gathered around him to help him get through the surgery. Of his forty-six family members, only two had asked her how she felt, even though she was swollen from the reaction for days. They had descended upon the house en masse after his surgery, seven of them staying the weekend. They had come from Mexico to show their family support, and as she had made up beds, gotten towels and necessities for those who needed them and made them breakfast the next day, she had been resentful, even while pretending to be appreciative of their support. At the time, she hadn't slept eight hours in thirty-six, and she had been hurt that no one seemed to care. True, they had helped her to make breakfast before leaving. It had been another moment when it was clear who was family for them and who was not. Blood was family, she wasn't. They looked after blood, not her. She was to look after them; they had done their part by showing up, showing themselves to be a good family, *"una familia unida."* It was one of the things she had admired about them until she realized the cost of that loyalty to everyone else. It seemed that everyone understood their code except her. She was the problem; she was the one who came to their world with different ideas, different customs, different beliefs. She saw and questioned their traditions and customs. No one else did. Shakespeare wrote over six hundred years ago that, "Custom then, is the great guide of human life." She fought custom and its ingrained, unquestioned, dogmatic and unchanging guidelines. Nacho and his family embraced it.

As she stared at the wax dripping down the ankles and feet of the sandaled candlesticks, she remembered again their first dance, her first dance with Nacho, and how she had tried to "find her feet" in the dizzying pace of the music, how her choice of those sandals had changed her life trajectory. If she had worn high heels, her world would have been very different. Would now be very different. She wouldn't be sitting here in this house, in this chair, looking at the fire and the burning candles. So, for a pair of sandals, her sandals, her life and Nacho's had been joined, and her life had brought her here. All for a pair of feet in a pair of simple sandals.

We go through life stumbling and falling and stumbling to our knees, and struggling and falling some more, making asses of ourselves... because we neglect or refuse to learn the truth.

Chapter SIX

THE MEMENTO

She sat at the desk in the kitchen, writing one of her never-ending lists. As she stood, up she noticed the miniature pewter clock on the bookcase shelf. It was a replica of the Birk's Clock in downtown Vancouver. Her mother had given it to her to remind her of "home." But Vancouver wasn't "home" anymore, Nogales, Arizona was.

> **It is this room, in this town, where my body finds itself.**

Vancouver was a place she visited. It had been a June night, a personal milestone she now measured time by, that marked the date she recalled by that small memento. That night she had changed and never gone back to what she had been before. That June night it had been slightly cool as the sun began to set.

It had been ten o'clock, but in Vancouver, the long days were one of the advantages enjoyed by the tourists who thronged the city in the summer months. Downtown, and especially Robson Street, were packed with visitors into the early morning hours. Robson was illuminated at night by the brightly-lit storefronts that housed clothing boutiques and shops selling other luxury items. Chocolate shops, coffee bars and souvenirs drew the crowds and their money. Street performers entertained the passersby, as the shops stayed open late to entice more customers inside their doors.

She and Nacho had parked, leaving her purse in the trunk of the car so that she could stroll around unencumbered in the crowds. They were nicely dressed, more so than was appropriate to strolling on Robson at night, but they hadn't bothered to change after their dinner out. They had come down to Vancouver after spending the weekend up at Whistler. They had gone to spend a few days alone for their anniversary. He had been hard pressed to take time off from work, but she had made it clear that it was important to her. It was their twentieth anniversary, and she needed to talk to him. There was so much that didn't work in their marriage. She felt like it was dying, that what she had felt for him when they first met was unrequited. It felt as though she was the only one who invested effort to keep their relationship going. He took her, and it, for granted. She had wanted some time alone with him to talk to him, tell him how urgent it was for them to somehow reconnect. To keep their marriage alive before it was too late. She remembered shutting the door to the hotel room and Nacho pulling her against him as she had released the handle. "Don't." "Don't what?" "We need to talk." "Later." "No. Now." He had been impatient. "What?" "Nacho, something is going so wrong. I feel like there's something missing that I can't get back. I've never felt like you really want to be with me. It's as though it's just convenient that I'm around, but you don't go out of your way to spend time alone with me." "Well, I'm here aren't I?" "Well, there we go. Who arranged it? Who had to argue and convince you to take off time to come?" "God, it's never enough for you. I'm here, we're away and you still complain." She started to cry. "*Nacho, conquista me. No siento que me quieres ya. Nunca hay tiempo, nunca hay romance. Siempre soy yo que estoy emujandote, jalandote, para que estamos juntos.*" He hadn't understood how serious she was. How tired of fighting for a relationship that he took for granted. He had kissed her and been oblivious to the desperation in her plea.

> The supreme happiness of life is the conviction that we are loved; loved for ourselves.

Now as they moved through the crowds, he took her hand, tugging it when he wanted her to change direction or avoid an on-comer. It annoyed her that he controlled where she walked. She wanted to stop for a crepe at the small creperie up ahead. It made crepes in the authentic style of France, wrapping their chocolaty or strawberry insides in soft, savory dough. They were served in a wax paper cone out a streetside window, so that they could be eaten walking along the street. There was a crowd of customers waiting for their orders at the take-out window. Spanish, Italian, Chinese, French and other languages mixed together in a mellifluous, multicultural blend, as the diversity of ethnicities were brought together by the desire for the flavourful crepes being prepared. Orders were often communicated by gesture, a universally understood language.

Her turn came to pay and pick up her order. Nacho passed her some money. There was a dark man at the register who spoke with a pronounced accent. He looked her over quickly and, noting her sophisticated appearance, asked where she was from. She replied that this was where she was from originally, but that she now lived in southern Arizona. He looked at her hand as she extended her payment. "What a beautiful ring you have on." "Thank you. It is my own design. I design jewelry." "It is very striking. Your ring is lovely," he commented, taking her hand for a closer look. They spoke a few more words before he released her hand, a pleasant, friendly connection in the noisy, congested crowd. Nacho looked at her as she bit into her crepe with satisfaction. This was one of her favorite treats, her taste for chocolate and sugar satisfied. "Have you been here before?" he asked. "Not this time," she replied. "This is my first crepe this time." "I don't think so," he said. "That man seems to know you pretty well." "Pretty well? I've never seen him before." "He was pretty friendly for someone whom you've never met before. Anyway, I know you're not telling the truth because I asked Stephanie, and she said that you've been down here already." "Stephanie is a child who is unfamiliar with the names of the streets. We only bring her here every summer. Neither is she a liar, nor am I, and I find it very strange that you are asking our daughter where I've been, so that you can check up on me." "I wasn't checking up on you. I just don't understand why you won't admit that you've already been here. What are you hiding?" She stopped eating her crepe and stood still. Time seemed to stand still. It felt as though the crowds pushing around and past them were from another time and place. A dreamtime. She couldn't even hear the noise of their chatter or the traffic, couldn't feel them brush against her and jostle her. Everything was still. She stood and looked at him. He moved forward, then noticed she had stopped. "What?" "Don't ever do that again. Ever." "What are you talking about?" "You know what I'm talking about. Don't ever talk like that to me again. I don't deserve it. I am not a liar. I am not doing anything I shouldn't, and I don't like the way you imply that I am." "I didn't mean it like that. You always take things the wrong way."

> **Believe nothing of me save what you see.**

She thought of the countless, futile arguments over the years. Six years of brief holidays together and twenty years of marriage made twenty-six years of stupid, pointless arguments, bad feelings, tears and recriminations. She had been doing this for twenty-six years. Twenty-six years and she was only forty. "Don't you ever talk to me like that again. I want you to apologize." The crowds pushed past them both. They faced one another, the two of them standing still. The dark evening continued its progress; the people continued on their way; the shops and cafes continued to serve the crowds. She didn't move. He looked uncomfortable and annoyed. "Come on. Let's go. What do you want?" "I want an apology." "Well, I'm not giving you one. I didn't say anything wrong. You're the one who won't admit what you've been up to." "I'm not going anywhere until you apologize." They had started to move with the motion of the crowd down the street. The eddy of people moved them along in a human current past bright shop windows, enveloping them both in the chatter of English, Spanish, Chinese, and the languages became one continuous flow of human gibberish. She couldn't distinguish what she heard anymore, she wasn't listening, she wasn't aware of anything except that this was not all right. She was blindly walking along, her uneaten crepe cold in her hand. She stopped. There was a stone bench next to some plants. She saw a garbage can next to them. She walked over to the trash bin, threw in the crepe, looked at Nacho's back as he walked down the street, and then sat down.

> **A living and not a dying body... will have... an incarnate will to power, it will strive to grow, spread, become predominant... Because it is living and because life is simply will to power.**

"I wonder how far he'll go before he notices I'm not with him," she thought. "He won't notice that I'm not with him for awhile, maybe at all, maybe until he gets to the car. He's going to be mad." The cold concrete chilled through her thin skirt. There were some homeless people sitting a little farther down. She was cold. She didn't have her purse or she would have taken off her jewelry and hidden it in her bag. Some passers by turned to look at her; she could feel their looks at "the attractive, elegant woman sitting by herself." She didn't care. She sat, and waited. She wasn't sure for what. She just waited.

Suddenly Nacho startled her. He stood in front of her, glaring at her. "What do you think you're doing? You're going to get mugged here. I walked all the way the car! Get up and let's go." "No." "What do you mean, no?" He was practically apoplectic. "Get up and let's go. You're being ridiculous." "I don't care. I'm not going unless you apologize." Every order he barked at her, made her more determined not to back down, not now, not ever again. She wasn't going to feel bad for something she hadn't done, not ever again. Somehow they both knew that this apology had a lot more invested in it than this moment. He wouldn't back down. That meant backing down for a lot of things. That meant being culpable. That meant he had been wrong. That meant she was right, and since he was the man of the house, the man in this relationship, since he had never been held accountable, he wasn't going to start now.

"If you don't come with me right now, I'm going to go without you." She thought of the fact that she didn't have any money with her, not even a quarter for a pay phone, never mind money for the bus or a taxi. She thought of the fight that was coming when they were eventually alone, and she knew that she wasn't going to fight again for some imagined behaviour of hers. Unless he acknowledged his abuse, unless he acknowledged he had treated her unfairly, this was the last time. She knew it was the last time.

> **That thing is called "free" which exists from the necessity of its being, and is determined to act by itself alone.**

She looked at his furious face and calmly said, "If you don't apologize to me for what you said, I will never get in the car with you." He saw that she was cold, afraid and determined. Very determined, strangely determined and unequivocally determined. He had never seen her like this. She had never been like this. She wasn't sad and hurt, she wasn't angry either. They were both shocked, she as much as he by her attitude. This was it. He turned and left her, crossing the street, disappearing into the crowd. She looked after him for a moment, then sat back down on the cold, concrete bench. She didn't consider following him as she wondered how to find a quarter.

As she looked at the small pewter clock from Vancouver, she thought of how much she had grown since that evening two years ago. It seemed like the growth rate of a newborn baby, rushing through its period of mewling dependency to get to a place where it wouldn't be defenseless anymore. She wasn't defenseless anymore either. She had grown, learned to look after herself, and learned to recognize and address situations that were detrimental to her. She had taken a long time to get to that place, but the difficult journey had made her stronger, more able and given her faith in herself. She picked up her list of things to do and moved to the next room.

To be coopt up as it were in a mockery of wedlock, to a perpetual betrothed lonliness and discontent.

Freedom... the most used word of our time... nothing more obscure, more ambiguous, more abused.

Chapter SEVEN

The Books

She pushed the heavy-paneled door inward, and crossed over the hatched pattern of warm brown wood, entering the room that contained her most valued objects: the study. The shelves and shelves of books were both home and escape to her, and had been since she was old enough to read. Whether living in Canada, Mexico or the United States, when her mind was inside the pages of a book, she lived her own reality. In this room were the childhood books that she had brought with her from Canada, the many novels she had read, the books of poetry, the books of history, the books of travel, philosophy, mythology, fairy tales, books on science, music, language, art, design and health, self-discovery and improvement. She had returned to university after twenty years of being auto didactic because she was happiest when reading the literature that taught her about the threads of human idiosyncrasies that wove themselves into every person's personal journey. She understood herself and those who touched her life better through the stories and poetry she read.

> **To be a Columbus to whole new continents and worlds within you, opening new channels, not of trade, but of thought.**

The study had two levels, the walls downstairs, bare of books, were hung with framed fossils, fragments of antique Buddhist manuscripts, copper engravings, illuminated calligraphy and exotic butterflies. Downstairs, the books were stacked in piles, piles on and under tables, as though they grew out of the surfaces they rested on. She walked over to the cast-iron, spiral staircase that lead up to the cases of books, winding her way up its wooden risers, peering at shelves of books in front of her as she reached the top. There was a Victorian phrenology head sitting between the books high on one shelf and a bust of Socrates on another, gazing outward from the books that framed them. She had placed the heads there to symbolize the power of the mind, nestled amongst the books that had illuminated, educated, befriended and nourished her own as she sought the infinite, the transcendent and the absolute within their pages. A grandfather clock ticked on another shelf, its musical chime on the hour a steadfast reminder that whatever she learned or created, there was impermanence to her endeavor, that she was a human being with a finite amount of time to learn and achieve her aspirations. The macabre visage of a bronze skull resting on a stack of books looked at whoever came into the study face on. Its empty sockets and barren form were without a history, without a name and without a face. The skull was her feared and acknowledged destination, a reminder that the form of the head, be it of Socrates, a theoretical map of the mind, or her own flesh and bone, they were in the end, just casing, a bony casing that was more permanent than the miracle of infinitely intricate workings housed therein. Words outlived a brief human passage. The words in the books that surrounded her were proof that a capable, eloquent mind, could leave a mark on the world that outlived a lifetime.

> **Many a man lives a burden to the earth; but a good Booke is the precious life-blood of a master spirit, imbalm'd treasur'd up on purpose to a life beyond life.**

Here, in her loft, she had found freedom that was uncontrollable and immeasurable, a liberty to go anywhere she chose. Up the spiral staircase, removed from the rest of the house, the panels and shelves of dark wood wrapped the walls and took her to a place where she was released into worlds created from the printed word, worlds of possibility transporting her to another time and place. Her sensitivity to discord and her insatiable thirst for knowledge had been the catalysts that drove her to lose herself to the world around her, nourish herself with the printed word, and solace her mind and soul within the ephemeral world of books.

> **My thought is me: that is why I can't stop. I exist by what I think... and I can't prevent myself from thinking.**

For years, when the children were small, she hardly read any books, just stacks and stacks of magazines that she could get through quickly, because, when she began a book, the world fell away, and her small children had needed her to be present. But the printed word had always, through the years, even before she had married and had children, been irresistible to her. Anywhere she found printed material, she was drawn by its power. Flyers, magazines, romance novels when she was young, book after book after book on horses when she was a child. She remembered her pride at seven, the day she had stayed home and read her first Walter Farley, a book over two-hundred-and-fifty pages from cover to cover, in one day. She had never found a useful outlet for her reams of horse knowledge, but it was there in her mind like so many other things she had learned, waiting to be tapped. To read was as necessary to her as breathing and eating. So many books.

> **The love of learning, the sequestered nooks, and all the sweet serenity of books.**

Her mother would take her to the public library, where she would check out stacks at a time every week, and to the local Five and Dime, where she and her sister bought the piles of comics that ranged from *Archie and Jughead* to the classic fables and fairy tales. The beautiful illustrations of those comic book classics were still a part of her cerebral and artistic reference library. Her mother had bought her first book, an illustrated Walter Farley, *The Black Stallion*, when she was five. She remembered clearly that it had been nighttime, that it had been a small cramped bookstore on Granville Street; how special that book had been because it was her own and she had chosen it for herself. She had been a passionate collector and avid reader ever since, and she was most content in this world wherein she strove to satisfy her insatiable thirst for knowledge and information. Socrates had wisely understood that the nature of the human condition needed self knowledge to flourish, and said so long ago with the maxim, "The unexamined life is not worth living." Within those words she saw her own value system reflected; the search for knowledge and truth was never a destination, but an ongoing journey that intrigued and nourished her spirit every day.

> A man may perform astonishing feats and comprehend a vast amount of knowledge, and yet have no understanding of himself. But suffering directs a man to look within.

She thought of the different moments that had made an indelible mark on her. Buying her first book, reading her first novel, and also the moments that had driven her to defend and fight for the right to read and learn what she chose. She remembered her mother's condemnation of the stacks of comic books she and her sister spent hours reading, her scathing criticism of the reading material as she carried them out to the yard and burnt them in a bonfire that lasted for hours, even as she remembered her encouragement to read Jane Austin, Leo Tolstoy, Dickens, Kazantzakis. It had been her mother who had taken her to the library, to the bookstore, the person in her life who always had an open book on her nightstand. She vividly remembered Nacho's anger when he had found her reading a romance novel soon after they married. She had held it in her lap to read in the car, and he had torn it from her hands and thrown it out the window of the car, furious, yelling that it was corrupting her to read trash, that he wouldn't have her reading polluting garbage because she would become as immoral as the characters in the book.

> Would you allow your wife... to read this book?

She had defended her right to read what she chose, refuting his right to control what she read, but it had been years before she accepted that his customs and beliefs would never be on the same as hers, years before she read words that expressed her belief that all knowledge was good.

> To the pure all things are pure, not only meats and drinks, but all kinds of knowledge whether of good or evill; the knowledge cannot defile, nor consequently the books, if the will and conscience be not defiled. For books are as meats and viands; some of good, some of evill, but the choice is to each man's discretion.

Nacho's simmering resentment when she returned to university, his unacknowledged anger and resentment, revealed itself in a hundred moments, situations and expressions that hurt her and eroded their relationship, carving a final epitaph upon the tomb of their marriage.

> A fool will be a fool with the best book.

She had returned to university because, after years of teaching her small children and sharing information and knowledge she acquired with her husband, she was starved to be in the company of individuals who could teach her what she was hungry to know, people who could respond to her questions, not just listen to them. Once in the classroom, all the reading she had done over the years finally found a place where it could transpose itself to an interconnected pathway of knowledge, each morsel of history, literature, theory and fact sustaining and complementing the next in her personal journey to self-fulfillment.

> The value of education... is not in the learning of many facts but in the training of the mind to think something that cannot be learned from textbooks.

At last, her final semester had arrived. Because of her decision to divorce earlier in the year, it was the first time in her three years at university that she couldn't lap up the information she was fed. Words seemed to slide off of her. As she tried to deal with all the overwhelming issues involved in the dissolution of a marriage, the dissolution of the world she had known for almost all of her adult life, trying to assimilate what she was learning in class was sometimes too much. Even so, there were moments of pure joy and inspiration when she read thoughts that illuminated her path to a life of peace, love and self-empowerment, an empowerment that she would never have achieved in the oppressive world she was emerging from.

As a Canadian, when she read Jefferson's words that "all men are created equal" with the right to "life, liberty and the pursuit of happiness," she knew that those words were about her too. When she read *Rasselas*, by Samuel Johnson, she recognized her indefatigable journey to try and unravel her life's purpose. When she read John Milton's words on *The Treaty of Divorce*, they resonated within her, his personal beliefs, so beautifully written, echoed her own when he stated that marriage was the union of two minds, not just two bodies, and that to negate that most primal and dignifying aspect of human union was to make humans no better than unthinking beasts in an bestial union for procreation's sake. Milton's pages and pages of prose reedified her in their affirmation of liberty free from oppression, human rights free of hierarchy and the rights of the individual to live a life according to personal doctrine. These words had an immediacy for her that were profound and empowering.

> **The pursuit of knowledge for its own sake, an almost fanatical love of justice and the desire for personal independence.**

When she had applied for her transcripts from the University of British Columbia with the idea of returning to school in Arizona, she had had no idea how far the journey would take her. The first day she had found out that she would be able to attend in the fall semester, she had called her son Thano from the middle of campus, sweaty and crying from running around all day to get all the papers submitted and told him, "I'm in! They're going to let me into the university! I can go back to school!" "That's great, mom. I'm really proud of you." They knew that he spoke for himself, not with the collective voice of the family. They had both known, without acknowledgment, that his father was not going to be pleased, and it had been only a few days later that he had said to her, "You know that this is only going to make things worse." And it had. Nacho had been resentful and angry that, not only her business, but now school as well, was taking her away, his effort to contain her thwarted again. She would drive an hour and a half to Tucson from Nogales every morning with Stephanie, leave her at school, then rush to her own classes at the university.

That first day of class, sitting in an auditorium with a hundred-and-fifty students almost all her son's age, she had been inspired to hear, "You are here to read literature, and in the books you will read this semester, you will find all the knowledge that humanity has produced, because mankind's journey and knowledge eventually finds its way to the printed page, to a book, in a book where we can read it and learn from it." She had gotten goose bumps listening to her professor's words, and felt a physical impact at being in a place where the possibility of all she could desire to learn was available to her.

She sat down at her desk and looked around the room that had been her refuge, solace and escape.

Some of the books that surrounded her were the texts she had read in the last three years. Chaucer, Milton, Woolenstonecraft, Aristotle, Welty, Winthrop, Keats, Dickens, Gosse, Carroll, Kristeva, Woolf, Yeats, Jefferson, Shakespeare, Melville, Einstein, Thucydides, Da Vinci, Trollope, Ruskin, Camus, Benjamin, Wilde, Foucault, Wordsworth, Paine, Bergson, Pope, Cooleridge, Sartre, Proust, Eliot, Bronte, Vasari, Plutarch, Beauvoir, Sydney, Locke, Donne, Hong, Kingston, Marlowe, Swift, Poe, Adorno, Theroux, Steinem, Freud, Defoe, Orwell, Kant, Hardy, Miller, Heraclitus and so many more.

> Knowledge thrives from exercise.

She understood how impossible it was to have learnt so much and remain the same person she had been when she began her voyage. She had been unable to accept the truths of tradition offered to her by her parents, Nacho and his world. She had challenged them, tested them by reason, and often found them wanting. She had fought to stay afloat, adrift, this new world she was determined to find just out of reach, swimming without direction but determined to survive. There had been no going back; she would drown. She had to take the words and ideas that floated about to build a life-raft. She had no choice but to follow her destiny and survive. The books that surrounded her were filled with words men and women had written, thoughts that could, would change someone's mind, or hopefully, many people's minds, about what the world was made of and who we are, why we were here, what we were meant to be, how we could honour our humanity. Fighting ignorance.

> Interested men who are not to be trusted, weak men who cannot see, prejudiced men who will not see.

Sometimes she would be reading ferociously along, only to stop and realize that the curious symbols in front of her eyes represented sounds to her, and those sounds, words, and those words, meanings, concepts, beliefs. It seemed incredible that these small black markings on a paper page could affect her so profoundly, but they did. She saw whole worlds in her mind's eye created by these little black symbols. Whole worlds.

This was the room that had been most important to her in the design of the house. This room and the kitchen were the fonts of nourishment that were indispensable for both herself and her family. It was curious to her that none of the children had her ability or love for either the vocation of learning or cooking. Even though she left books in all their rooms and had gifted them books she thought they would find interesting since they were babies, the boys only read under duress and necessity, and while Stephanie loved books, it was without her own passion and voracity for knowledge.

Nacho bought books constantly and had begun to read them off and on, but he had never finished one in its entirety since she had known him. He wanted to read but couldn't do it. She had always felt that her constant reading was a point of annoyance for him. She had shared her reading with him constantly over the years, recapitulating stories and books of information, but he had never been interested enough to read them himself. He didn't seek or pursue knowledge, but casually acquired information. Her experience had shown him to lack a deep respect for learning unless it produced monetary reimbursement in some way.

When the children were small she would try to read to them at night before they went to bed. Many of the shelves in the library were full of children's stories that she had given them. She had taken drama in high school, and used that training to read to the children with a southern accent, a witch's voice or mimicking any character that suited the story plot. The boys had especially enjoyed her storytelling when they were small and had hung on her words with delighted expressions. Stephanie had begun to collect books early on and it was still one of her favorite things to do, to go to the bookstore, any bookstore, repeating the pattern she had established with her own mother.

There were times when she really had to hang on to her belief that the cost of her education would be worth it in the end. All the soul searching, the insatiable quest for knowledge, information and understanding, the days of trying to study and learn while it eroded her marriage had been irreversible steps forward. Even as her studies conflicted with her children's schedules and limited her own ability to come and go as she pleased, she had been determined to finish. She had puzzled and sometimes irritated family and friends with her mission to get a degree, irresistibly drawn to seek knowledge. The thirst in her drove her to free herself from the desert she was in and find her way to survive. She saw learning as the land of plenty: the well she could always draw from to slake her thirst. Nirvana.

The aroma of wood, rich with wax, married with that of paper and leather. These were the scents of comfort, her books, this room, friends and partners in a way a person never could be. She looked around at her friends and acknowledged her need of them as well as her joy in their company.

Nacho had feared their power too, had always known that in a battle for supremacy he would lose. They were the irresistible addiction that had finally drawn her away from him, the lover he had feared all those years when he tried to keep her to himself, closed off from the rest of the world. He tried to control her in every way possible, but hadn't been able to control her mind. He hadn't even been able to meet her there, and that was how he had lost her: to the paper words and bindings that had taught her that:

> ...words are a form of action, capable of influencing change.

The ephemeral world of knowledge that blew through her mind had changed her more than any material world ever could, and had taken her away.

> All that we are arises with our thoughts. With our thoughts, we make the world. We are what we think.

Chapter EIGHT

The Gifts

Awaking, she pushed aside the down comforter encased in Egyptian cotton and French lace. The creamy silk sheets felt soft against her feet as they slid out of the bed and onto the cold limestone tiles. It was Christmas morning, and she wanted to get the treats into the stockings before her children awoke. Her children, no longer small, were twenty-one, nineteen and fifteen now, but they still claimed that the stockings were the best part of Christmas. It felt good that her months of searching and collecting on their behalf were appreciated.

As she padded into the bathroom on bare feet, she passed the chair laden with her gifts from the night before. A Gucci coat, Prada shoes, Luis Vuitton sandals, silk nightgowns and a soft wool shawl were some of the presents she had received from her children and husband. They had watched her reactions as she took off ribbons and opened boxes. They had wanted her to enjoy her Christmas. The children had looked at her and then at their dad, watching their interaction. They well remembered the years she cleaned up after they had opened their stacks of presents, setting carefully aside her few presents, ones she had purchased for herself. Tears had often been in her eyes as she tried to make sense of their lack of effort to buy her anything. This year they had made a team effort of it, trying to help their dad out with participation and advice, guiding him in the art of gifting she had taught them.

At first, when they were newlyweds, he would buy her a piece of jewelry every Christmas on Christmas Eve. Ten o'clock at night, the twenty-fourth of December would have found him at his brother-in-law's jewelry store, choosing a piece for her. If he couldn't buy her a piece of jewelry worth thousands of dollars, he wouldn't buy her anything at all. When she had been less than thrilled with his expensive, last-minute purchases, he had stopped buying her gifts. The children hadn't noticed at first, but as they got older, her eldest son began to ask his grandmother to help him with the purchase of a purse or pajamas for his mother. But he knew, and she knew, that he was trying to make up for his father's lack of participation.

Slowly, over the last few years, as their relationship became more strained, he had begun to buy her gifts again. This year was going to be different. He and the children had planned for her, just as she did for them. Her husband, sons and daughter wanted it to be perfect. Decorated with hand-carved wood ornaments, glass icicles, dolls, little houses, clear, bright, little lights that faded on and off and a bright red, green and gold ribbon that spiraled from top to bottom, the tree was as beautiful as ever. "The most perfect Christmas tree I've ever seen," a guest had remarked one year. A beautiful tree, a delicious dinner, presents stacked up under the tree; they were very fortunate. They were fortunate and unfortunate, and they all knew it. There had been a lot of stress this year, a lot of unhappy moments and tears, and this was the time to make up for it all.

> **Where men lived in careless abundance, knowing and heeding nothing of that trust, which, for her, had been turned to bitterness.**

She had tried on the coat, commented on the shoes, smiled and kissed everyone, pretended to be happy, far more pleased to watch her children open their gifts and exclaim over the surprises she had wrapped in tissue and bright paper than she cared about opening her own. She had bought him gifts too, but the joy of giving him something special was gone. It was obligatory this year. When everyone was done, the last box, a big, square, heavy one was left. The office had received it that morning and had sent it over. It had been wrapped and put under the tall tree with her name on it. She peeled back the bright wrapping paper and opened the carton. "It's the dictionary that I ordered! It's here!" Her sons and daughter looked at her happy face. "Look what Mom gets excited about." They shook their heads and smiled at her pleasure, while Nacho's expression betrayed his realization that his gifts hadn't produced the effect he had wanted. The books she had ordered for herself were what she really enjoyed. She could tell that he had tried, that there had been an effort to be thoughtful and buy her things she would appreciate, but something was gone, changed, and he knew it.

He had ordered, wrapped and helped the children with the shopping and had even bought poinsettias for the house. He had sent a driver from the office over to put Christmas lights up for two days, had gone with her to buy evergreen wreaths for the front doors, and hadn't complained when she hadn't produced her usual batch of Christmas cookies that were his favorite. He had made an effort as never before. There had been a quiet Christmas party at the office in the afternoon this year, instead of the usual restaurant venue. He hadn't played the role of the jovial boss or father that his sons brought home in a stupor at three in the morning. They hadn't hosted their family Christmas party at home, with he, the benevolent, drunken, host letting the last guest out the front door in the early hours of the morning, either. He had done everything right this year and she could see how much he had tried. It was too late.

> **Giving with one hand and taking with the other is deluding, not giving.**

As she put on her new Italian robe and slippers, she looked at the bottle of medication sitting on her dressing table. It was the same table she had used as her childhood desk, sent from Vancouver, now painted with ribbons and flowers. The doctor had advised her to try these pills. She had decided to start today, Christmas Day, so that she would have time to adjust to the medication before the holidays were over. The pills were an anti-depressant; the doctor hoped that it would help her. She tried to resolve her feelings about a life that required medication for her to get through it, about this Christmas morning, as she took half a pill and washed it down her throat with water from the carafe on the vanity. She looked at her reflection in the mirror framed in mahogany. As she splashed water onto her face from the swan-necked faucet, the water ran over her skin in pseudo tears, down her cheeks into the dark green marble sink. A poem she had read last year in her poetry class came to mind:

> O plunge your hands
> in the water,
> Plunge them
> in up to the wrist:
> Stare, stare in the basin,
> And wonder what
> you've missed
> O look, look in the mirror,
> O look at your distress;
> Life remains a blessing
> Although you
> cannot bless.

It was Christmas Day; her children were all home, sleeping in their beds. They were together, they were a family, and she had orchestrated another great Christmas experience for them and for her parents to enjoy. Her younger son had helped her cook Christmas dinner, her elder son had washed all the china, crystal, silver and linens, and her daughter had set the table and carefully decorated it. They all wanted the illusion to be a reality; everyone wanted to believe the handsome picture they made, but she felt it was her responsibility to keep this family a family, whatever the personal cost. And the cost was very dear.

She turned to leave the bathroom, the ferocious face of the spouting gargoyle above the tub staring at her departing back. The smiling faces of her children looked on in innocent happiness from their childhood snapshots in her Venetian mirror frame, the engraving next to the mirror of the three children, two boys and a girl playing with little birds, a constant reminder of why she was here. The clock on the wall continued to mark the passage of time as another day, another Christmas morning, another year evolved as she stepped across the limestone and green marble tile floor, out the door, past her slumbering husband. Voices faintly murmuring recriminations followed her, insisting, cajoling, that she make real, something that was only possible in the imagination. Her children didn't want an illusion; they wanted it to be real. She didn't want an illusion either; no one had tried harder to make the illusion real than she.

And her husband was finally trying. Wasn't that worthy of keeping it all together for everyone, for the better good?

> For there is no place that does not see you. You must change your life.

She padded quietly down the hall, the navy, cream and rose wool of the Persian runner muffling the sound of her footsteps as she passed her daughter's and both her son's rooms. Family members watched her walk past them from the colorful picture gallery on the walls. They were the most reproachful. Who would they be, who would they belong to if she failed? As she opened the great iron gates that separated the bedrooms from the center of the house, the mirrored panels of the gates trapped her in their reflection, in the hall, in the house, in this family, in this life. The present, the past and the future were capturing her in the mirrors, the angled refection of one door within the other allowing no escape, like a carnival mirror that lead to nowhere and to infinity at the same time. That was her world, the world she had created for herself.

She moved past the mirrored trap and slipped silently down the stairs into the center of the house. The ghosts of the twenty-six foot trees that had died shadowed the center court. They had towered to the ceiling creating an energy, a truth that was now dead and gone. What better illusion than a created garden, an artificial interior garden in the middle of a desert, to prove how capable she was? But the beautiful trees that had comforted her had been no more capable of surviving in artifice than she had been. She had fought for years to save their lives, bringing every known expert to salvage them, putting artificial lights in their trunks to help them survive the lack of natural light and feeding them every suggested nutrient. But the air and wind that were meant to ruffle their leaves, warm their beauty, nourish and feed them had been absent. They had struggled valiantly, their trunks oozing sap as from a human wound, gumming the floors with their distress, their leaves falling daily, denuding them of protection and an ability to nourish themselves until there were no leaves left. The trees had been taken out one by one as they lost their struggle for survival. The fourth and last trunk had been removed just before the Christmas tree had gone up. It had been dead for two years but had been left there as a reminder to her of what could have been. Only the weathered, wood planters bore witness to their existence. She had wanted to create an oasis for herself in every way. The trees, the fountain which never played anymore, the flowers, the paintings, had been a solace for a heart and mind that were hungry for more, a spirit deprived as the desert landscape outside the walls. She had been determined to create what was not there, determined to create abundance where there was dearth, but determination had not been enough.

> **Nothing will come of nothing.**

She had loved that the high ceilings and stone floors reflected the sound of the splashing water throughout the house from this verdant core, delighting in the musical sound the fountain created. When Nacho would get home, he would go directly to the switch and turn it off. It annoyed him in every way. The sound of the water, the wet floor around it, the waste of money to keep the small motor going, those were the things he saw. He railed against the plants that she loved, never bought her the flowers she so enjoyed, unless on a day of token tradition. One day, finding the fountain off again, she had shouted that it was a metaphor for their marriage, that he didn't care if she enjoyed it or not. All that mattered to him was that he didn't like it. She had tired after that and only turned it on for visitors, one more thing that others saw as perfect in this beautiful home, a delightful accessory that was a silent witness, as were the ghostly trees.

> **Nothing can ensure me against myself, cut off from the world and from my essence by this nothingness.**

But it was Christmas morning once again, and she filled the stockings of her children as though they were children, and not grown young adults, trying to create another illusion of the perfect Christmas morning for them. White chocolate angels, cinnamon gum, imported chocolates of every variety, exotic lip balms, specialty hair products, and even a special box with a jewel made by her, were packed into the same stockings that "Santa" had once filled after eating the cookies and milk. She had a sackful of goodies that she sorted through, carefully putting the same items into the green bag with the teddy bears, the red bag with the Scotties, and the navy bag with the white, bowtied geese. They were finally full to the brim and she set them artfully on the huge, tufted, velvet chairs next to the fireplace. Later that morning, one by one, her sons and daughter shuffled into the room, sleepy from a late night and the effects of a rich turkey dinner. She watched in delight as they sniffed chocolates, lip balms and small bottles of cologne with the same gestures and habits she had watched define them from the years when they ran in with red sleepers and tousled hair. As usual, Nacho missed the best part and wandered in when they were done, sitting on the sofa, watching TV, the excitement of Christmas morning already fading. Both her brown satin stocking and his Victorian needlepoint spat never had anything in them. They were just decorative Christmas accessories, token stockings to show the children that they were a family.

She remembered reading:

> **Real giving means choosing, expending time, going out of one's way, thinking of the other as a subject.**

It had resonated within her and she had written it down on a Post-It and stuck it on her desk, a daily reminder of what giving meant to her. When she did something for her children, her husband, her friends and family, it came from her heart. It wasn't about the intrinsic value of the object or gesture, but the pleasure that object or gesture would bring. It meant making their favorite soup, writing them a note and leaving it on their pillows, it meant unconditional love. With her children there were no conditions, with Nacho the list was so long it ran into pages, shaped by the codes of possession. Never before had it become as clear how confining those codes were, and how antithetical to her way of being. They were codes that would never let her grow, but always hold her in check. They were not built on trust and understanding, but on a reluctant relinquishment of power and authority that she never accepted and always fought. She knew with absolute certainty that all the slippers, rings, purses, paintings, gloves, coats, nightgowns and necklaces could never make up for the lack of freedom and integrity to live her life on her own terms. In this relationship her right to be the proprietor of her own person and capacities would always have to be fought for. Nacho didn't understand that freedom lovingly nourished and fostered would only create more love. Control, criticism and anger at her every evolution had atrophied the love she had felt until it was a dead thing, weighing down her spirit. In this relationship she was only another object that he possessed, a living, breathing prize that was nice to look at, a good cook, a good mother to his children. After all these years he still didn't appreciate or understand the essence of her, which was why he didn't know how to give to her in any way. He had once said of her, "If there is a big boulder in front of you, you hit it head on, over and over and over again instead of just going around it." "But if I can find a way to break it down, if I have the spirit and the ability to change that route for myself and others by breaking it down, isn't that good?" "You just don't know when to quit," he had said. "You want to change the world, and it's not going to change, no matter how hard you try." That had been one of their defining moments as a couple. He had made it clear he didn't appreciate what others saw, and what she saw, as personal valor and perseverance. He saw those same actions as blind determination and stubbornness. She wanted him to applaud her efforts, encourage her to reach for the stars, break down the boulder. But the more she accomplished, the more unhappy he was, weighing down her every joy and success with dour expressions and negative comments. The positive remarks were so overly self-conscious they lost all meaning for her, begrudgingly learned and begrudgingly expressed as she, the marriage counselor and their children tried to teach him to be a better partner.

The more different from oneself the other experiencer is, the less success one can expect with this enterprise.

She wistfully remembered their first Christmas together at their little house on Carrillo Street. She had been so young and pregnant with their first born, Thano. Their little home had been the size of an apartment. Nacho had connected the new lamp in the kitchen and hung the shelves in the laundry himself. They had just moved in the month before and had cardboard boxes for nightstands, a new sofa and table for the living room. There had been one small closet they shared, the size of hers alone before she married, and a tiny bathroom so small only one of them fit inside at a time. They had lived in that house off and on, with an interim of five years in Mexico, before they built this home. That first Christmas she had put up a tiny tree, just for them, just two feet high, that she had decorated with one string of lights and a few ornaments that hung on the elegant tree in the foyer now. She had given him one gift and he had told her that hers was pending Christmas Eve, in Culiacan, with his family. They had been happy to be together, just the two of them, in that little house with neither of their families and no children. It had been a lifetime ago.

> **What is time then? As the future it is possibility; as the past, it is the bond of fidelity; as the present, it is decision.**

♦ ♦ ♦

She sat down in the big chair empty of stockings and waited for him to open the door. It was the eleventh of January. The Christmas ornaments were all gone now, put away for another year in storage boxes stacked one on top of the other in the basement of the house. She had stopped taking her pills after a week. Her naturally vibrant energy had been on simmer for six days, her interest, appetite and attention for everything and anything placated and dulled. She had become apathetic and tired, napping in the daytime when she usually only slept five or six hours a day. She had told the doctor, "If this is what I need to get through my life, why don't you just give me a lobotomy, like Jack Nicholson in *One Flew Over the Cuckoo's Nest*?" They had both laughed to diffuse the serious intent of her comment, both knowing she was near crisis as her torn feelings about her life rocked her emotional tranquility every day.

> **When reality becomes unbearable, the mind must withdraw from it and create a world of artificial perfection.**

As she waited with the music from *Chariots of Fire* playing around her, filling the house with its soothing music, she thought of what she would say. She should have, could have, waited for a more opportune time to tell him, but one of her failings was her unequivocal straightforwardness. She wasn't diplomatic, wasn't evasive and wasn't manipulative. Life seemed so much easier for those who used those tools. But she couldn't live in the same house as him, share his room and their bed without telling him how she felt. And she felt so sad. So sad to end this marriage that had taken twenty-two years of both their lives. Twenty-two years of love, resentment, compromise, laughter, passion, solitude, anger, disillusionment, pain, tears, sadness, impotence and finally acknowledgment. There was only so much she could do and the rest was not up to her. No matter how determined she was, this boulder could not be broken down.

When she had begun to go to therapy, her doctor had sent a test she had taken off for analysis. Some scientific lab in the Midwest had analyzed her answers and responded with a scientific measurement of her character. It had been fascinating to her that her character, or lack thereof, had a concrete value that could be referred to as a point of fact. Reading down the scores, she saw that she had the lowest possible inclination to addictions of any kind, that she had the ability to read character as astutely as a law enforcement agent, and then the most fascinating element had come up. "What does this score mean?" she had asked her doctor. "It means that, metaphorically speaking, if you were a boxer and you got knocked down, you would get up, and if you got knocked down again, you would get up, and if you got knocked down again, you would get up. You would continue to try and get up until you were practically dead." She had immediately recognized the truth of his words. Her husband had made his own reading of her character without the scientific evidence. His metaphor of her bashing herself against a boulder that was in her way, instead of going around it, was just as valid. Was her character going to change? Probably not. She could modify her behaviour through her understanding, but her natural inclination would always start from that point, as would his when he couldn't accept her the way she was, that he couldn't smile and cheer on her idealistic nature, but only belittle and stifle it.

The first and most innocent lesson of nature is to turn away peaceably from that what afflicts and hazards our destruction.

Weeks earlier, on the first day home for the holidays, her younger son had found her in the kitchen. Leaning on the counter he had said to her, "Mom, let's have a peaceful Christmas. Please don't bring up your feminist stuff about women's issues and women's inequality and all that stuff. You know how it upsets Dad." She had looked at him without replying for a moment and then said, "What do you like about our marriage, Nick?" He looked at her steadily and replied earnestly, "That you want to get old together, that you want to see your grandchildren play together in your home, with us around." She later said to him when he had reproached her for not being happy, "Nicholas, I've tried. I've tried everything. You know that. The counseling has helped both your dad and me, whether you agree with counseling or not." "Yes, it did," he agreed. "You guys are much better." "The counseling helped us to have a better relationship, Nicholas. It couldn't save our marriage," she had gently replied, forewarning him as much as she could at the time.

She had felt so sorry that he wanted it so badly, so badly he wanted her to want it too. She had known clearly in that moment that her spirit would die if she had to continue to fight for its existence for the rest of her life. He was a good son, a wonderful son, as was her eldest, a wonderful son, and her daughter, the joy of her life. They would have to understand that this could not be done, and that it wasn't for want of trying. It just could not be done.

> Suffice that to me strength is my bane.

She heard Nacho's key in the lock and the alarm bell pinged, signaling his arrival. He walked out of the hall with his suitcase in tow, back from another of his ubiquitous business trips. His daily phone calls with her over the last week had been almost formal as he described his efforts to establish the new office in Los Angeles. She too had been polite and asked the right questions as a million thoughts flew through her head during every conversation. When should she tell him? How should she tell him? Was this the right thing to do? Was this going to be better, or worse than what she already had? Would he be angry? How angry would he be? Would he be vengeful, physical? Would he be sad? Would he be resigned? Now the moment was here. He walked up to her and she stood and kissed him. "How was your trip?" "Oh, fine, you know, long, as usual." She thought of his effort to begin this business in Los Angeles, of how hard it was for him because she had insisted and insisted that he begin to diversify in the United States instead of depending on the family holdings in Mexico. She wanted their sons to have something for themselves here too, options that they could use to expand the family business for themselves. He had finally done it, but it was too late.

The fireplace flickered behind them both, the golden flames creating only a facsimile of warmth. The lights of the city shone in the distance as the darkening blue twilight of the evening cooled the paned glass of the french doors, keeping the night air out. "Nacho, I need to talk to you." He stood still and waited for her to continue.

> By frequently forcing a mixture of minds that cannot unite.

"Nacho, this is not working, and no matter how much I want it to work, it doesn't." She started to cry. The tears ran down her face, wetting her shirt. Her voice was choked as she continued. "You and I are so different, and it's not just that we're different but that you want me to be someone I'm not and I want you to be someone you're not, and we are never going to be those people. It's an illusion to think that we are and we are torturing each other, destroying each other, in our determination. We didn't want this when we married. How did it become so ugly, so destructive? I realize that I can't do that to you any more, and I can't live in a marriage that does it to me. It's over. It has to be over. I still love you. I will always love you. You were part of my life for twenty-nine years, but it has to stop. I have to go. I want a divorce."

His face froze, then shock, hurt, bewilderment and confusion played over his face in quick succession. "Did you tell the kids yet? Have you told anyone else?" She was amazed that those were his first questions, as though she was supposed to take care of everything as usual, while at the same time, she was relieved that he wasn't angry. "I haven't said anything to anyone; I wanted to talk to you. I don't want you to be angry. I'm so sorry, I'm so sorry," she sobbed, her shoulders heaving as she embraced him. He automatically held her, their embrace familiar, the feel and smell of each so familiar to one another, while they both somehow registered that this would soon be different. "I want us to be friends, Nacho; I want to be able to call you or you, me if we need something. I want to celebrate our children's birthdays together and yours and mine. We can still be a family, just not a couple. We can do this. Nobody has to follow any rules about how this has to be. We will make our own rules and we can make them work."

"Yeah, sure," Nacho said. "We will, sure. It's okay." She couldn't believe he was trying to comfort her. She sobbed louder and louder, gasping for air as the pain she felt and caused, overwhelmed her. All the past injustices and injuries didn't matter at that moment. She didn't feel a gram of anger, justification or retribution. All she felt was remorse and an overwhelming sense of sadness and loss. Her illusions, the illusions she had fought so hard to preserve were dying a tortuous death inside her, ripping her apart as she let them go. His shirt was soaked with her tears as she sobbed and sobbed. "If you want to do this... " "I don't WANT to do this. I have to do this. I have to do this, Nacho. It's not going to work. We just have to accept that we are not suited to one another and move on. We're still young. We can make our lives over again. But not together. We don't work together. We created three beautiful children together. That will not change. They are the best part of both of us, and they are wonderful. We have to stop this though. We've done too much damage already." His face was bereft. "I know," he said, both of them remembering their daughter's tears as she reproached him and fought for herself and her mother a few days before. That had been her epiphany, that moment had engendered this one, and they both knew it. It had never been as clear as on that day how indomitably divided they were, and that there was no meeting point, not now, not ever. It was as though they were communicating in two different dimensions.

She had finally quit. She had heard that the marriage is over when the woman no longer wants to try, that it's the woman who puts the most energy into the relationship. That was probably true most of the time, and in her case it certainly was. There was no going back. She had made a decision and she was going forward. She had the rest of her life ahead of her, even though at times she felt so old and resentful that the best years were gone, wasted trying to make a marriage work, a love survive, a life valid. The best part of the past were her children, and that made it worth it. They were healthy and whole, bright and beautiful, and they would never want for her love.

She had read something that gave her solace, something that she was not the first and only to understand what their relationship had lacked. She too understood that she needed a soul mate, not a bedmate or someone who provided her with an excess amount of material wealth. Three Christmases ago, she had given him a framed piece of illuminated manuscript that explained what the essence of marriage was for her. She had read it to him because it was in old English, but he hadn't really digested the full import of the message or the gift. The pale green parchment framed in gilded gold had the medieval image of a man and a woman with their hands raised in a pledge to one another in the center of the script. It read:

> **Two are better than one; because they have good reward for their labour. For if they fall, the one will lift up his fellow: but woe to him that is alone when he falleth: for he hath not another to help him up. Again, if two lie together, them they have heat: but how can one be warm alone? And if one prevail against him, two shall withstand him; and a three fold cord is not quickly broken.**

A three fold cord. They had been married three times, once in Mexico and twice in Canada, two civil ceremonies and one in a church. They had lived in three different cultures and countries and had given life to three beautiful human beings. The three fold cord was not easy to break; it had taken years and years of wear and tear to destroy its strength. Now the cord was frayed and broken, a sorry remnant of what could have been.

Thano had left home days into the holiday, saying he needed a break. He had had an altercation with his father and was putting distance between them to deal with it. He had called her, knowing that she would be upset that they weren't all together. "It's not real, Mom. We are all pretending to be this family that we're not." He adored his new girlfriend, whose parent's divorce had scarred her. "Natascha wants to be with our family because she says that we're a real family, that she misses that." "Thano, do you want her to love you for what she wants you to be or for who you are?" "I know. I know, mom. It's just that I want to make everything perfect for her. I want to give her what she missed." "Our family is not perfect, Thano. I know and you know that people look at us, the house, the cars, all the beautiful faces and think that we have it made. Our lives are not perfect. We have all gone through a lot. We are all scarred and human, Thano, with the same problems, shortcomings and failures that many share. It's okay. It's allowed. She will love you anyway, even without the perfect family."

As she and Nacho held one another, she knew that this moment of empathy wouldn't last. Anger and recriminations, accusations and insinuations were going to come flying her way when he had a chance to digest what had happened. But, for the moment, they were for a rare moment on the same page. They were both mourning their loss, sorrowful that they hadn't been able to succeed in keeping their marriage together, that they hadn't been able to make the illusion real, that they hadn't been able to build a happy and harmonious home, that they hadn't been able to love each other, as man and wife till the end of their days, as they had promised at the beginning.

This room, this home had been built on a dream of possibility, and those dreams had been tortured and burned till they were ashes in her mouth. She knew that the house had to go. It wasn't fooling anyone; it wasn't a dream home and they weren't a dream family. All of it was real and flawed. They were just human.

Chapter NINE

The Kitchen

Her hands moved quickly, chopping onions for the soup she was preparing on the butcher block counter that anchored the center of the kitchen. Softly suffused with sunshine from four skylights, the kitchen was the room that had demanded the most from her. She had intended it to be the heart of the house both conceptually and physically, and it was that. It wasn't anchored against a peripheral wall, as in most homes, but at the core of the family room, the breakfast room and the more formal dining room, feeding all of them, as she did her family and friends, from this central source.

The thread that runs from... a simmering pot... to the past traditions and future life.

Food had been such an important part of her childhood and youth. Her parents had both grown up poor and often hungry in pre-world War II Greece. They had also both come from farming families, families whose livelihoods depended upon the bounty of the earth, the clemency of the skies. Her father had come from an island in the Aegean where they grew almonds, olives and some vegetables to get by. Her mother's family was from the Peloponnesus and had grown potatoes and grains. Food was, and continued to be, an important part of the lifestyle in Greece. She remembered being in New Orleans and how a native had explained to her what a large part of the local culture food was, a throwback to the French heritage of the area. He had said that it was an ongoing competition, that women, men, families were very generous, often asking strangers home to share in their hospitality so that they could show off their culinary skills.

> **Food is still love and food is still culture, tradition, and pleasure, still the raw material of artfulness.**

"Peopls'll ask'n you's how's you like'n de's cook'n, and dey'sa meani'n it. Dey's want's to know's how's it's tasti'n, which'ns 'da best you's eve had and why'sn so's dey's can compares it. And if'n you's sayy's that you's had anuthu recipe that you's likin, tdey's not hurt like, 'cause the's wants t' knows so's they's can improve lik'en what dey's cooks. Its meanins a lot here's hoe good'n a cook you's is."

> **To invite people to dine with us is to make ourselves responsible for their well-being for as long as they are under our roofs.**

The Greeks weren't much different. It was fiercely competitive as to whose recipes were the best, and most of the men cooked just as well as their wives, except for the fussy sweet things that were seen as frivolous. In terms of hospitality, cooking was a key element in the Greek way of life and a strong part of her family traditions as well. It would have been untenable to have food catered, or simply not to feed a guest to excess, in her home. Only a very bad mother did not feed her children well, with home-cooked food. No Greeks she had grown up with would think of take-out food or frozen dinners as a solution to a meal and even Oreo® cookies were frowned upon, just as prefabricated food of any kind was "junk."

> **How we eat our food reflects our husbandry of ourselves... we are what we eat.**

Their family had moved to Osoyoos when she was six, her father having bought a restaurant that he saw as a financial opportunity. The town of Osoyoos straddled a small lake that nipped in and out to form three bodies of water that nestled at the bottom of a valley, its hills covered with orchards and vineyards. The restaurant, sat on a spit of land with views of two sides of the lake, the bridge in front of the restaurant connecting the one side of the lake to the other. Under her father's and mother's ministrations, it soon became famous for its food. Her father had not known how to cook professionally when he took it over, and very soon afterwards, it began to look as though they would not be able to keep the restaurant going. No one came through the doors and it was losing money hand over fist. Afraid that he would lose everything that he had to his name, her father threw out the cooks. "If I'm going to lose my shirt, I'll do it myself. I don't need you to do it for me. I can cook too. Just let me learn." And he did. Growing up poor had been the best training possible, teaching him how to buy well, and his Greek heritage was invaluable in learning how to buy what was fresh and flavourful. Meats, fruits, vegetables, chickens, turkeys; they were in the middle of a cornucopia in Osoyoos. He would drive around to the different farmers every day and fill up the trunk of his car with supplies for the restaurant. This was a man who had trapped sparrows to eat because his parents sometimes didn't have any food to put on the table. He felt as though he had walked into the Garden of Eden. Though she and Angela were small, they were extra hands to be put to work to pick cherries, apricots, peaches, plums, apples. She remembered learning to distinguish the transition of summer to fall by the fruit that hung ready on the trees. The majority of the farms were full of immigrants from Germany and Portugal. Their farming skills were impeccable and their fruit stands sold vegetables grown from their own small plots, as well as honey from their own hives and syrup made from their own fruit. Her mother would sometimes take them to the orchards, and in the shade of the acres of trees, teach them to find and pick the wild asparagus that grew under the bowers of fruit-laden branches.

> **The immigrants... who would no more have been without fruit trees... than without shoes or a roof.**

Her parents were very wary of leaving their two young daughters alone, even with the amount of time the restaurant demanded of them. So they put them to work. In the summer, they spent days in the kitchen peeling peaches for the homemade fruit pies the pastry chef would produce. Her father would buy the overripe fruit by the case, immerse them in huge buckets of hot water to loosen their skins, and then sit her down with, Angela and the "Three Musketeers," their male cousins from whom they were inseparable; they would all groan in unison when they were brought a fresh bucket to peel, desperate to finish their work so that they could go play at the beach, in the lake, for the rest of the day. Their fingers would be pruny from the hot water before they were done, and peach fights were often the highlight of the day.

> **Rise early. Eat simple food. Take plenty of exercise. Never fear a little fatigue.**

In the winter, she and Angela would often go with their father to the restaurant in the morning before school. The lake would be covered with ice, the windows cold with frost when they would enter the kitchen and watch him light the stoves, stir the simmering stock pot, and fire the gas burners for the day. They would carry the comfort of those scents with them as they walked out into the biting cold air, to walk along the frozen lakeshore on the way to school.

She recalled eating chicken noodle soup and grilled cheese sandwiches at the pullout cutting-board table. The family sat around the Formica table with her dad at the head, as her mother placed the food in front of them in steaming bowls and plates. That was home, the kitchen of her first home on 16th in Vancouver, red linoleum floor and white enamel refrigerator, the smell of bread baking in the oven, her mother in the kitchen.

> **The wife and mother which is the fountain of wholesome love... in parlour and kitchen.**

When they moved to Osoyoos, home became the restaurant. The chef, the pastry cook, the waitress: they were all part of an extended family that had watched Angela and her grow up. She was young when she learned how to mix pastry dough, make apple crumble, butter stacks of toast, make stock, whip eggs and fry an omelette. She learned of the satisfaction to be gained by serving good food, food that customers preferred to their own home cooking. She learned that food was a common language which brought people together, be they customers, family or friends. It was a legacy passed on to her by her mother, by her father, and by people who had learned to do it for a living because they loved it. It showed in the way the chef cleaned off the edge of a plate before putting it out, the way the pastry chef beamed when customers came back again and again for her deserts, and the way her father and mother took pride in a business that nourished others even as it nourished their family.

The joy of living wrapped up in the delights of food.

The restaurant also taught her how to work hard. There was no other choice. When the tables were full, and there was a line-up of people waiting to come in the door, tempers hung by a thread, and often the thread snapped. Running the restaurant under that kind of pressure wasn't fun; it was hell. Her parent's marriage changed. Their roles had been defined before the restaurant; her mother had been at home with her children, their father went out to work all day. Before Osoyoos, she remembered home as a safe, comforting place and the kitchen being at the heart of that. When her mother went to work with her father, home was where they went to sleep, but as a family, they were together at the restaurant. Her mother and father began to argue. The tension over making the business succeed, the need to produce the food for the customers quickly and efficiently when the restaurant was busy, the stress of working together all day began to erode their marriage. But it was more than that. Their roles weren't clear anymore. Her mother worked with her father neck and neck; more so, because the responsibility of the house and the daily routine of her daughters were hers as well as putting in her time at the business. She had an opinion of how things should be done, as did her father. But he was the "head of the house," so he wanted his opinion to be the one that counted. Her mother resented the lack of respect for her abilities, work and contribution. The fights became an almost daily event.

Happiness too swiftly flies.

It didn't just change their relationship, it changed her world. Whereas before she had her mother to come home to, now she often came home to an empty house, a latchkey child before the phrase existed. Osoyoos was a small town, and the walk home after school often took a detour to the swing set at the beach, a walk through the orchards, and a stop at the corner store to buy candy or a soda. She developed a friendship with a girl at school who liked to get her work done as fast as she did, who was kind, and more often than not, she would end up at her house. She became a surrogate sister; they had an uncommon affinity, in that they were equally sociable and intellectually capable. They both loved to sing and sang in choir together, played soccer after school together and shared the same perspective on what was kind or unkind, good or bad, as well as a passion for reading. They were both "good girls," without the social stigma that often implied. When she moved back to Vancouver three years later, it was as though she had to leave her family, because her friend had in so many ways become that.

To like and dislike the same things, that is indeed true friendship.

The relationship she saw between her parents, their ongoing battles, the lack of respect she saw in their relationship, left scars. She learned to fear the word "divorce" as though it were the bubonic plague. No matter how bad things were, it wasn't an option. She learned that she hadn't seen how to build a partnership. She knew that her parents loved one another and that they shared many traits— intelligence, drive, kindness, love of family, generosity and incurably romantic natures— but they just "didn't know how to communicate," a point her father reiterated ad nauseam.

She remembered standing outside the small bookstore on Main Street Osoyoos with her mother one day, looking through the window at a display of doll furniture. She had turned to her mother excitedly, "Mum, could I buy that furniture to play with? It's just the right size for my Barbies." "You don't want that furniture. You're too old to play with dolls. You're not a little girl anymore." She had been crushed. It wasn't just that she wasn't to buy the furniture; it was that she couldn't be a child. She was eight. It was instantly clear to her, not that she wasn't a child, but that her mother didn't want her to be a child. If her mother acknowledged that she was dependent, that meant she needed to sustain a different relationship with her; if she insisted that she were old enough to be self-sufficient, then there was nothing wrong with leaving her alone to look after herself. She knew that her needs were being sacrificed to salve her mother's conscience. It was her mother's way of dealing with it. She had to be old enough.

The consequence was that she felt as though she had been denied the right to her childhood, a feeling exacerbated by an early growth spurt. She looked like a teenager at ten, and was therefore treated like a teenager, losing another five years of childhood. As a child, she had never felt that her parent's didn't love her, but she had felt that they didn't have time for her. She was very conscious of not repeating the mistake. She put her children first until she felt as though she didn't have a self. Part of the way she took care of her brood was to feed them. She had learned that lesson from her family as well. Food came from the heart, it was a gift to nourish, create traditions, and build memories.

She put the onions in the pot and began to chop carrots, celery and parsley.

The ongoing conversation with her parents revolved around whether Thano, Nicholas and Stephanie had been fed or not, and what. When her parents visited, her father planned his day around his grocery stops, and he always arrived from Vancouver with ice chests full of sea food, feta cheese and Greek olives. When her parents took her and the children to Greece with them one summer, the children's most pervasive memory was of the mountains of food they were unrelentingly fed by relatives. They still groaned at the memories of platters of food they had tried to eat in order to show appreciation for their relatives' hospitality.

Some people use other than physical food to assuage their hunger— money, sex, social status, etc., but still the simplest comfort is palatable food.

Nacho's birthday was in the fall. As she had seen her mother do for her father, she would invite friends and family to celebrate, covering the table with food she had prepared for their guests. It was her gift to him. Even when she had been in high school, she had been infamous for her cooking skills, bringing cheese straws, almond paste strawberries, even cheesecake she had made, to their teenage house parties. The first boy to like her gave her *Gourmet's Basic French Cookbook* as a Christmas present when she was fifteen, two weeks before she met Nacho. She hosted sit down dinners for her friends, making the appetizers, bread, main course and several deserts. She loved to cook.

To be without a sense of taste is to be deficient in an exquisite faculty, that of appreciating the qualities of food, just as a person may lack the faculty of appreciating the quality of a book, or a work of art. It is to want a vital sense.

Even now, with her world changing every day, with the future as uncertain as it was, she found such comfort in the creation of a dish for her sons, for a friend. She really had no need to cook for herself, so she made meals for others, giving herself the creative outlet that she needed, giving to them something more intimate than anything she could buy. Cooking them a dish or a meal was an authentic gift that came from within her, feeding and nourishing them, her life force ingested. It was also an offering, a gesture to show her appreciation for friendship, to show her love to her children by making manifest a marriage of flavours that she carried in her mind.

You give but little when you give of your possessions. It is when you give of yourself that you truly give.

Even though her children no longer needed her to nourish them, it was a simple act of continuity for Thano, Nicholas and Stephanie, when everything else about their family was changing. These were familiar tastes that were their past, a past that they could take with them wherever they went. It was their story as a family as much as where they had lived. The chicken soup, rice pudding, roast lamb, refried beans, bread pudding, were hearth and home in their minds. She knew that, but had to teach it to them. Just as they were creating a new present with an unknown future looming in front of them, so they could hold onto the best of the past with comforting associations that carried no connection to strife, unhappiness or ill will.

A meal however simple, is a moment of intersection. It is at once the most basic, the most fundamental, of our life's activities, maintaining the life of our bodies.

She heated the pot and let a patty of butter melt to a sizzle. Then she added the skinless chicken thighs.

She looked around at the kitchen as she stirred the browning chicken. She had designed the soft maple cabinets to look like furniture, creating a room that could have come straight from an English country house. So much of what she had learned from working in the restaurant kitchen was incorporated into its functionality, her ability to create the aesthetic, into the design. The boys had just this year begun to show an interest in learning from her, calling to ask for recipes, calling their grandmother to ask for hers. Subconsciously, they were building their own archive of family records. Thano had even gone to Nogales and taken some cookbooks from her collection. It was instinct that drove them. If their mother was absent, who would keep the traditions alive? Who would tell them how to make the food that was their family heritage? Curiously, Stephanie showed no domestic inclinations; it was the boys who were interested in learning the craft.

> **Our kitchens tell stories of who we are. They reflect our values and our dreams. And they remain... the best possible place to share.**

She added the vegetables, browning the ingredients together, making the roux.

Her mother and father were great cooks, as was Nacho's mother. His father had taught his young bride many of the traditional Greek dishes from his homeland, as well as her own country's traditional recipes. Their family had grown up on those flavours until each of them, in turn, married. The Mexican cuisine became a part of the family repertoire, along with the influx of other family traditions. The comfort, joy and importance of a flavourful meal was important to all, a common thread that wove through all of the families, a language that joined them together as Spanish, English or Greek could not, in a hybrid tradition that all appreciated and fed themselves upon.

It was the room that everyone first migrated to when they entered the house, drifting over to the stove to lift the lid of the pot and taste what simmered inside. It was the room that attracted the most people when she hosted a party, groups standing around to get a taste of what was coming out of the oven. It wasn't a room they had spent time in, as a family, as much as the others. The kitchen didn't have a table where they could all sit down, just a counter for a snack or a light meal. It was where the food came from, but not where they gathered. When at her friends, it was where they always sat, around the kitchen table, telling each other stories of who they had been, their histories as women, as daughters, as wives, as mothers. How often had their voices been raised in laughter or broken with tears as they struggled to make sense of their destiny, their burdens and their gifts, sitting around a kitchen table that was the heart of their homes.

It was in this kitchen that preparing food had become a burden. She had created the problem by her nature to be efficient, overly generous. It was the metaphor for her marriage as well. She had thought that she was capable of doing all of the work herself. She had finally tired and asked Nacho to participate, but by then, he didn't know how. She was the one who had always done it all, buying the food, preparing it, serving it, enabling him.

It takes two to make a marriage a success, and only one a failure.

It had been another recipe for disaster, assuming all of the responsibility to make the marriage and the kitchen work, one of several in their marital cookbook. But, she had created this burden for herself. What she had created in the kitchen was always an act of giving. It was not reciprocated, but always flowed from herself to them, a constant stream that transferred itself to her children, her husband, friends, and guests, those that worked in the house. It was an unrelenting responsibility. To feed them, always giving, giving, giving. She had read that the person who is a giver does not give unconditionally, as they may think that they do. Somewhere in the back of his or her mind, in the subconscious, is the hope that the gift will be acknowledged and reciprocated. When it isn't, the giver feels unappreciated, used, and eventually, resentful. As soon as they feel resentful, they feel guilty, because the act of giving should be unconditional and isn't supposed to require reciprocity. Then they feel ungenerous by compromising the "gift" with unacknowledged terms. So, to compensate for feeling resentful and guilty, they give again, and again, and again they become the architects of their own disaster. If they don't recognize the pattern and change it, it will be a never-ending cycle. When she and Nacho began the counseling, their responsibilities in the kitchen became one of the dynamics in their relationship that did change. Nacho began to help out by making breakfast on Sundays, washing the dishes at night, taking out the garbage, sometimes buying groceries: small contributions that helped her to feel that he was participating in a task that had been exclusively her domain. Before counseling, even on "downtime," weekends, when everybody else in the family got a break from their routine, she was the one expected to produce something for the family to eat.

Give us this day our daily bread.

She found herself becoming angry when she made breakfast, angry when she washed the dishes, angry to be in the kitchen at all. It became a chore instead of a gift. She had begun to feel like the family servant, and Nacho's participation helped her to feel that her work was acknowledged, the burden of responsibility, shared.

> **A crust eaten in peace is better than a banquet partaken in anxiety.**

When they first married, Nacho had enjoyed her cooking; it was her one ability that he wasn't intimidated by or resentful of. Eventually, it was often criticized as, "Too salty, oily, spicy, greasy." It upset his stomach. What had she put in it? Why didn't she cook *frijoles*? Why did she cook bean soup if she knew that it didn't agree with him? Why did she cook what he couldn't eat? Didn't like? For the last three years, even though she prepared food daily, he would come in late and not eat anything, intentionally rebuffing her one part of the family responsibilities by not eating, implying that what he contributed was indispensable and that what she did, was.

She had purposely designed the kitchen without a place for all of them to sit down, because that way, she had thought, they would be forced to sit down and eat together. It had rarely happened. Nacho had usually come in late at night after everyone had eaten, and a family meal was more often in a restaurant than at home.

> **What's the good of a home if you are never in it?**

When her family had moved back to Vancouver from Osoyoos, dinner was always eaten together, in the kitchen, with a family discussion about business, news, school, politics or family issues, as part of the daily routine. In her family, nothing had been verbotin; her parents had included Angela and her as equals in everything under discussion and had listened to and respected their conversational contributions, even when they were small. Her parents had only lately reverted to being authority figures in their old age; as young parents, their daughters always had their attention when they had something to say.

> **People... revealingly use culinary customs as... indications of a culture.**

She added water to the pot, about halfway up, added salt, pepper, a bouillon cube, a cup and a half of rice, and turned up the flame to bring it to a boil.

She, Nacho and Nicholas had been in the kitchen together, standing around the counter late in December of 2002, discussing which showing of a movie to see in Tucson later that day. Thano was not there; he had left after an argument with his father a couple of days earlier. They decided to leave immediately to catch an afternoon show, so as not to return too late at night. She went to tell Stephanie to get ready. "I don't want to go. Why do I have to go? You guys can go to the movies. I just want to stay home." "You can't stay alone. I'll stay with you." "Why do you have to stay? I'm going to be fifteen in a week. My friends stay at home alone. Why can't I?" "That's true. Other girls your age baby-sit and even have jobs. Nicholas and Thano stayed alone at your age. You're right. I guess you can stay. We'll be back by eight." She, but especially Nacho, had always been uncomfortable leaving Stephanie alone because she was a girl and because the houses in their area were not very close together, but she felt that her daughter was right. It was time to show her that she was trusted enough to take small steps at being responsible for herself. She walked into the kitchen. "Where's Stephanie?" "She doesn't want to see a movie. Let's go." "Well, if you don't want to stay, then I will." "It's not that I don't want to stay, it's that she doesn't want to go." "Yeah, right. I'll stay anyway." "That's not the point, Nacho. She needs to be shown that we know she can take care of herself." "She's not old enough." "Well when will she be old enough? She's going to be fifteen in two weeks." "I don't want to argue. I'll stay." "What does that mean? You don't want to argue, but we have to do what you want anyway? Why can't you respect your daughter's or my opinions?" Nicholas was getting upset listening to what he saw as the beginning of a feminist argument. "Stop it, Mom. If Dad wants to stay with Stephanie, let him. Let's go." "No. Stephanie needs to be allowed to stay alone in her house. She can do this. Nothing is going to happen. If she could baby-sit and be responsible for making a decision about a small child, she can take care of herself as well." "God, Mom! You always have to make things so difficult! Why can't you just go to the movies and let Dad stay?"

The soup began to boil. She turned it down to a simmer and covered the pot.

"Because it's not fair to your sister! How will she learn to be self sufficient? At what age, when? When she's sixteen? Eighteen? When she gets married?" "You're being silly." Stephanie had come into the room, sitting down across from her father. "Why can't I stay, Dad?" "I'm not comfortable, Stephanie. You think that you're old enough, but you're not.' "Well, all of my friends are old enough, and have been old enough for a couple of years. Why aren't I?" "They have different customs in their homes. I'll stay with you." "But I don't want you to stay with me. I want to be able to stay in my house by myself." "Why? What do you want to do that you can't do when I'm here?" "Nothing! I just want to be able to be by myself." "I'll stay." "Nacho. You're not listening to your daughter and you're not giving her a good explanation." "Mom!" Nick exploded. "Stop it! Let's just go! You're making such a big deal of it!" She turned to him. "How is it that I'm the one that's always to be corrected, Nicholas? Why isn't your father ever responsible?" "Well, he's not this time! He wants to stay with Stephanie, so let him stay. What's the big deal?" "I just explained and Stephanie just explained what the big deal is. You don't seem to be listening." "God, you're impossible!" "And you need to leave. This is between your father, Stephanie and me. You need to go." Nicholas slammed out of the house. Stephanie, who never cried, had rivulets of tears running down her cheeks. Quietly crying, she began to logically explain to her father why she should stay at home by herself. Nacho looked at her, heard her, but didn't listen. He had his own agenda running through his head. As she saw the mounting frustration on her daughter's face, as she inwardly applauded her ability to speak to him in a manner he could understand, and yet saw the continuing implacability in Nacho's expression, she thought that her heart would burst. She finally intervened. "Stephanie, I think that you should let your dad and I discuss this. Why don't you let us talk?" Stephanie turned to her with a look of determination on her wet face. "Don't you dare send me out of the room. My father is going to listen to me and hear what I have to say. Don't you dare send me away. This is between me and him." She couldn't watch. She left the kitchen and let her daughter try to communicate with her father on her own terms.

An hour later she walked back in. Nacho sat at the kitchen counter reading the paper. "Where's Stephanie?" "She went out with a friend." "What happened?" "Nothing." That had been her epiphany. She had looked at Nacho and understood that he had missed, absolutely missed, all of the significance of what had just transpired. She also knew that he would continue to do to Stephanie what he had done to her all these years, determinately suffocating her "for her own good." She knew the consequence of living that life. The consequence to herself had been to feel as though she were buried alive in a tomb, shouting at the top of her lungs for someone, anyone, to hear her, because Nacho didn't. Nacho never heard her. He was deaf to anyone's voice but his own. It was over. She couldn't live with him. In those few seconds, as she stood in the kitchen and looked at him that afternoon, her whole world changed.

She turned off the soup and walked out of the kitchen, turning off the lights.

Some things you can't see until it's too late.

Chapter TEN

The Crucifix

The tall, French-paned window illuminated the room, the small, green plants on the tables thriving in the soft southern light. She studied the Edwardian screen in the corner with its hand-painted, soft orange poppy panels, the petit point rugs in their pastel tones, the upholstered headboard with its checkerboard pattern in creams and tangerine, the tall, celadon armoire with its huge, gold keys and the gleaming dark wood of the Georgian antiques. It all created an ambience that was soft, soothing and obviously feminine. People touring the house would often stop short when they walked into the room, draw a soft breath and say, "It's beautiful. Does Nacho mind that it's so feminine?" She always found the question odd, her perception being that the bedroom was essentially a female sanctum, a space that was hers and that he entered.

Groupings of Christian iconography hung on the walls, gifts collected over the years. They were so numerous that she sometimes referred to their room as "the chapel." She herself found the androcentric dominion of religious teachings offensive and illogical. She had gone to a Catholic girl's school for eight years of her life and since then had released herself from the dogmatic and hypocritical dominion of the faith. "Popery" was the derogatory term that Milton had used for it, and with that she agreed.

Thano had given her a group of prints framed in black lacquer that were biblical images from the Old Testament, and the rest of the icons were principally from her sister, Angela, who had reacted to the Catholic schooling in a way opposite to her own. One plate hung on the wall was a rustic, beautifully hand-painted image of Mary with her small son, and below that hung a simple wooden crucifix, its ends capped with brass finials, that she and Nacho had purchased from an antique shop on their honeymoon in the south of Spain. She stopped and looked at its form, and remembering how it had captured her eye, that sunny day twenty-two years ago in the cobblestone alley of Marbella.

Last month, days after she had told Nacho she wanted a divorce, they had found themselves in their marriage counselor's office. The session had begun to go awry quickly as Nacho had made it clear that it had been the counselor's job to convince her to stay married, not his. As he became offensive, she had stood up in agitation and rebelled against the customs he was trying to impose on her regardless of her own needs or wants, regardless of whether the life he inflicted upon her made her happy. The image of the little brown crucifix had been in her mind as she turned to Nacho and emotionally said, "I knew I'd be crucified for this. Women in my world are not supposed to have needs. We are trained to put our children's needs first, our parents', our spouse's next and to ignore or bury our own, and if we don't, we are BAD women, unnatural and selfish aberrations of our sex who are abandoning our given mission in life. And we will be crucified accordingly. Well, I don't buy it anymore. I'm not an innocent, feeling guilty and unworthy of happiness anymore. I have only half a lifetime left to live, at best, and I'm not going to be a victim. I brought up my children, they will always be my children, but Nacho you are not the man I should have married. I know that now with absolute certainty. My life cannot be joined to yours anymore, and I will not be crucified for a decision I made in the best of faith when I was a child, twenty some years ago."

She had designed a crucifix for Stephanie for her first communion, a beautifully feminine piece of gold with a pink diamond shaped center stone, the arms of the cross accented with tiny green and white pearls and diamonds. The metalwork was pierced, imitating the nuance of lace in fine metal. Thano had asked her for a crucifix last year for Christmas and she had given him the bloodstone and diamond cross he now wore every day. Nicholas had gotten his this year and its Byzantine form was accented with champagne diamonds. They were opulent pieces, too much for their young persons, but she had wanted to give them a gift they would have for the rest of their lives, showing her love in the tradition of the European families with a piece of gold. They had no significance for her symbolically, just simple, symmetrical forms that were a reminder of her heritage.

She saw religion as a human catastrophe that destroyed so much more than it preserved, thinking of the words of Thomas Paine,

I do not believe in the creed of the Jewish church, by the Roman church, by the Greek church, by the Turkish church, by the Protestant church, nor by any church that I know of. My mind is my own church.

All national institutions of churches, whether Jewish, Christian or Turkish, appear to me no other than human inventions set up to terrify and enslave mankind, and monopolize power and profit... Every... church or religion has established itself by pretending some special mission from God, communicated to certain individuals.

The Jews have their Moses, the Christians their Jesus Christ, their apostles and saints; and the Turks their Mohamed; as if the way to god was not open to every man alike.

Just as dogma and tradition controlled the direction of man's religious belief system, so too had custom and tradition managed to wrest her son's belief system into a place unfamiliar to her. When the boys had demonstrated their anger towards her in the last couple of months, she had been devastatingly hurt. The last weekend, Thano, her "umbilical child," had come down to see her from Phoenix after evading her for weeks. He had ignored her cajoling that he see her so that they could talk. She remembered walking into the restaurant and the powerful feeling of love that had filled her heart when he stood up from the table to greet her. She was always amazed at the physical resemblance between them. His thick curly hair, his almond-shaped eyes with their long, curly lashes, the pointed shape of his upper lip, even his hands and feet, were very much her own, but in a masculine proportion. He had a very elegant and stylish persona as well, unusual in a young man of his age. "Hello, Mother," was his warm and habitual greeting, pushing in her chair as they sat down, his manners always so considerate. She looked at him with love and pride, saying, "It always makes me so happy to see you." "I know," he said. They began to talk, but as they had both known would happen, the conversation inevitably turned to the situation she and his father were facing. His face changed from being open and receptive to shut down and dismissive. He was not open to what she had to say. He didn't want to hear it. Thano, more than the other two, had been most affected by the cloud of unhappiness he felt emanate from her over the years. He had been very attached to her as a child and as a boy— the consequence of his love for her and his sensitivity to her unhappiness was an emotional intuition that was uncanny. His reaction to her now was unbearably painful and unexpected. She had thought that his support and understanding would be instant and unconditional, that her tall, beautiful son would rally to his "beloved mother's" defense. Instead, his taciturn demeanor showed his empathies to tend, if not towards his father, at the least not with her. He didn't want to discuss it, and she didn't know why, only that it hurt her like a bleeding wound.

> Every man shall bear his own burden.

The plan of buying groceries for the boy's apartment fell by the wayside as the afternoon progressed and his resentment to her overtures grew more obvious. They stopped at a take-out pizza restaurant with a charming outdoor patio, but he was increasingly sullen, and she, teary, as she tried to get through to him. Nacho had planned to meet them there, and Thano's face brightened when he saw his father, which hurt her even more. "I have to go," Thano said shortly. "I've got homework to do." Nobody suggested that this was an obvious excuse to get away from the tense and unnatural "family" get-together. She offered him the pizza to take home. He didn't want her pizza either. He kissed her and his father good-bye and walked off to his car, she walking sadly behind him since her car was in the same direction. He hadn't wanted to walk with her, and her throat ached from holding back the tears as she assimilated his intended rebuff. This was the little boy who had adored her. It was very hard to digest.

> Soul out of the night that covers me,
> Black as the pit from pole to pole.

That night, as she tried to run off her seething emotions on the treadmill in their gym, she finally had to get off as her mind and emotions whirled with the events of the day, trying to make sense of it all. She walked into the bedroom closet where Nacho was changing. He was getting ready to go off to sleep in Thano's room, as was his custom since December. "We did a great job, Nacho. We deserve congratulations and a golden trophy for doing such a great job. Why shouldn't our son be upset if we've decided to get a divorce after living in misery for twenty-two years? That's what we taught him. Marriage is miserable, it's about disrespect, unhappiness, loneliness and lack of communication. His mother taught him that. I taught him that I don't deserve to be happy as long as the show keeps on running along smoothly and everybody else's needs are met. All of a sudden, the rules are changed and he's upset. If I put up with it for this long, I should put up with it forever, so that, as I taught him, everyone else can have what they need. They can't accept that it's not my fault, because I'm the one who made the decision. I chose to say that enough was enough." She turned and walked out as he bowed his head and looked at the shirt in his hands.

She got back on the treadmill, but she was so distraught that she had to keep the pace at a slow walk as sobs racked her. The tears obscured her vision so that she kept on going by holding onto the handrail. She was keening the loss of her beloved son; images of his face as little boy, as a younger boy, as a child, as an infant, flashing through her mind. She felt a hand on her arm. Nacho took her by the hand and turned the machine off. She was crying so hard that she could hardly stand, and the irony that he was comforting her was not lost on either of them. She wanted to speak, but her tears wouldn't let her until finally she managed to say, "You don't understand. You can't understand how it feels to be so hurt by this person you saw come out of your own body. I'm his mother. *I'm* his mother. He's my son," she cried, her shoulders heaving in his grasp.

"I'll talk to them," he said. "I'll talk to them. It's not your fault. I'll make them understand."

Children begin by loving their parents; as they grow older they judge them; sometimes they forgive them.

The next morning she had gotten up early and gone to work in the kitchen. Nacho sleepily walked in later and looked at the various pots simmering on the stove. "Are you cooking?" he asked. "Aren't you ready?" she said. "Ready for what?" "Aren't you going to Phoenix to talk to the boys?" "Oh. Yeah." He packed the food into his car and she hoped for the best as she watched his car disappear up the driveway.

He didn't talk to her when he got home that night, and she could feel his anger. Whatever had transpired between her three men that afternoon, she would never know, but afterwards, Nacho's anger was palpable. She knew that that was the day he had lost hope of reconciliation. After that he was always angry. The boys talked to her more often, but their sympathy for their father was still obvious in comments like, "If I get divorced after being married for twenty-two years, I'm not going to give my wife half." "What about *your* vows, what about *your* promises. Don't they mean anything? What about commitment?" She couldn't imagine them saying the same things to their father, and couldn't justify all her reasons for her decision because that was an invasion of privacy between their father and herself. Time and anger at the injustice of the situation they turned a blind eye to eventually eroded her best intentions and spilled over into her conversations with them, spilled over and damaged her relationship with them even more. She didn't believe in prayer, she believed in the symbol of the Renaissance whose artists had been wise enough to associate and teach through art, that Time and Truth went hand in hand, and that Time would eventually vindicate her. However hard and painful it was, she had to wait for them to see with their own eyes what had happened to force her to make the decision she had. "Why now?" Thano had said to her "Why now after twenty-two years?" "Because it took me that long to admit that anything I was determined to do was not always possible. That as determined and driven as I am, it is not always enough. I cannot do more than my share. Sheer will and determination cannot fix everything and it took me twenty-two years to acquire enough humility to admit that." He hadn't replied to her.

> All that we send into the lives of others, comes back into our own.

Nicholas had come to Nogales from Phoenix one weekend and again two days after that. He was so hurt and so intent on being there for both his father and herself, as though that would make things better. He was so beautiful that men and women, young and old, turned to look when he passed, but she was always quick to point out that his greatest attribute was the kind interior not available to view. He had always felt the need to help those less fortunate, and now, those less fortunate were his mother and father. But it was his father he felt most protective of. When Nicholas was up in the study with her, he would leave, go sit with his father and watch television with him. When she went down, he would go with his father to the office. He seemed to feel that his father needed more support. When Nacho left for Los Angeles in September, he flew out to see him three times in five months, but he only visited her in the house in Tucson, once. She felt so alone, and sad that he didn't want to spend time with her, even as she knew that it was his choice and the best he could do with what he was feeling.

> To discover a new truth, one has to smash to atoms almost everything learned, and arrive at a new truth with hands blood-stained from the slaughter of a thousand platitudes.

He met her in Tucson at a little coffee shop she favored just as the sun was going down one day. There were a lot of things to be said and they sat outside at a small iron table under a blossoming orange tree. The pungent, aromatic scent of the orange blossoms scented the air. They battled into the night, as the scent became indelibly ingrained in her memory as a part of their story as mother and son, the son that was insatiably curious, heartbreakingly handsome; the son that had an innate kindness and who challenged her as an equal, a young man in the prime of youth with no quarter given for their difference in age. "I told Dad what I thought when I saw him, that I didn't think that it was fair for you to get half of everything or for you to get all of the money from the house." His perception of what was fair had already been influenced. She listened to him and knew that she would have an uphill battle to give herself a voice, and that she would probably never be truly heard. It wasn't just his father, but a whole world of tradition that she was fighting; a world he had grown up in, been formed by, even though she had been his mother trying to teach him with her value system.

If you can keep your head when all about you are losing theirs and blaming it on you.

She immediately thought of what Nacho's reaction to his son's words must have been and how they must have inflamed his righteous indignation, his traditional position— that in a divorce, annihilation was the best defense. In spite of everything his father had done, at heart her son perceived her decision to divorce as a betrayal. All he saw was that his father was now remorseful, alone, that he wanted her back and that it hurt him to be alone, to have lost his wife and the world he had known for most of his life. Nick's comments would have been like putting a match to gasoline. She saw that the task in front of her, rather than trying to negotiate any kind of amicable agreement between Nacho and herself, was going to be monumental and made worse because of the boys' attitudes towards her. She looked at her passionate young son and she saw him with the sad eyes of loss and love as she hugged him, kissed him and thought of his and Thano's actions and words in the past few weeks. Without conscious thought, the years of catechism brought the words to mind, "Forgive them, Father, for they know not what they do."

♦ ♦ ♦

She looked at the small, wood crucifix that she had bought so many years ago, before the boys were even born. The image of Mary in the plate above, holding her small son close in her arms, symbolized every mother's story. A mother's story is a story of a love so powerful it makes her vulnerable, subject to pain from loss; the loss of a son. The anguish maternal love brings every time a child is hurt or hurts never ends. The love, the great love children engender from the moment they become a part of a mother's body and her world, creates a unique vulnerability born of them, the children that are always held, close to her heart.

You have begot me, bred me lov'd me: I return these duties back as are right fit.

Chapter ELEVEN

The BED

Tall double doors opened into her bedroom. There, sun shone through the French paned-window, framed by heavy wooden shutters, and onto the delicate fern draped over a table in front of the bed. The bed was the focal point in the large room, with its inlaid, George V desk, its hand-painted Edwardian screen, its copper engravings of romantic symbols and landscapes, and the pale green loveseat facing the celadon armoire, with its hidden television and piles of folded linens.

The bed. It was the quintessential symbol of marriage in so many ways. In times past, even for her grandmother's generation, it was dressed with special sheets for a couple's wedding night, the bride and groom escorted to the chamber and bed to begin their conjugal life after the sexual consummation of their marriage. The sexual act or lack there of, infidelity or frigidity, constituted the basis of marriage for centuries. Mental compatibility, common interests, respect and love were all considered unnecessary accoutrements to the sexual act that was sanctified by the church and acknowledged by society as the all-important ingredient to guarantee procreation and genetic continuity. Institutions reduced human intercourse to the same level as that of the lesser beasts: an act of begetting.

Canon doctors made marriage a sacrament—not God.

Before she married, she had often read in bed all night, arriving sleep deprived at school the next day, the satisfaction of finishing the book before daybreak more rewarding than an extra few hours of sleep. Her bed was where she had listened to music in her room, day dreaming the daydreams of teenage years. When she was a small girl, she had enjoyed a twin bed covered with a simple coverlet in a room she shared with Angela in Vancouver. When she was seven, they had built their house on the lake in Osoyoos, and she had been given her own room. It still had two twin beds, but became her's alone. That was where she had read stacks of comic books and horse stories, novels, history books, *Good Housekeeping* magazines of her mother's that she found laying around, *Redbook*, and *Highlights for Children*. She would lay on her bed and read for hours with her turquoise, namesake parakeet sitting on top of the book, hopping in its sleep when she turned the pages, silently keeping her company.

They had moved back to Vancouver when she was nine, and she had been allowed to decorate her new room as she pleased. She had painted it pink and dressed her bed with a pink-flowered bedspread to match the drapes, the pink so bright her friends could tell when she was in her room because the pink shone through the drapes and reflected onto the white eaves outside the house at night. It had been where she read in bed all day on Saturdays and Sundays after getting up late, sitting amongst the rumpled blankets and flowered sheets without any responsibilities except to finish the book she was immersed in. It had been a very girly room with the pink paint, white furniture, tidy and full of delicate houseplants. Her stereo and bookcase had been full of her favorite books and music; the objects in her room were already starting to define who she was by the things she wanted around her.

Happiness too swiftly flies.

There were no books of her own in the room before her now. She didn't like to read in bed anymore, and hadn't almost from the time that they married. All the books were on Nacho's bedside table, but he didn't read them, he just collected them. The bed, with its creamy, Egyptian cotton sheets, its alpaca blanket, its lace-covered, down comforter and silk pillows was used only to appease her fundamental need for sleep. She didn't like to watch TV in bed, read in bed or even sleep in. The bed was always impeccably made up, even on weekends, the pillows stacked and fluffed in perfect order, the coverlet without a wrinkle, the sheets pressed and fragranced. Yet in spite of its beautiful and inviting accessories, the bed didn't invite her to lie down when she was tired; it offered no solace or refuge, or even a moment of comfort. For her it was a necessary piece of furniture, prettily dressed up with the right combination of sheets and covers to compliment the decor of the room.

> **To be coopt up as it were in a mockery of wedlock, to a perpetual betrothed lonliness and discontent.**

When she had been pregnant with Stephanie, she had been put in bed on medication for the last two months of her pregnancy as the doctor fought to keep the baby inside her as long as possible, fighting the premature labour that went through her in waves, the contractions steady for day and night for two months, the labour deterred by the medication. She had lain in bed day after day, only permitted to get up to use the toilet, or to shower, and it had even been necessary to shower sitting down. For a person who loved to be out and about, one with an irrepressible amount of natural energy, she had been both fearful for the health of her unborn child and helpless to do anything except follow the doctor's orders. She had lain for day after day looking at the ceiling and at the walls, uninterested in watching television or reading, just waiting for her child to be born. She had hated being in bed, had felt imprisoned, punished, helpless and responsible. It had been necessary to push herself into the background, to "disappear," so that the new life growing inside her could come into the world. It had been a necessary sacrifice, a willing sacrifice, in order to give life to the child begat in the same bed. She was the vehicle because the child she carried was worth the sacrifice.

When she and Nacho had first married, she had often lain awake, afraid to stir in case she woke him with her movements. She would listen to him snoring lightly for hours, sleepless, trying to accustom herself to sharing her bed with another person. It had not felt like her bed then; she had felt an intruder, not a partner. Only someone he slept with. It had felt like she was somewhere she wasn't supposed to be, their intimate relationship already contaminated by his jealousy, insecurity and control. The bed had created an unnaturally important connection between them as she sought love and comfort, he, validation and gratification. One evening a few years ago, Thano had come into their room after they had gone to bed, finding her asleep with her head on Nacho's shoulder as he watched television. Thano had commented upon it the next day, how he had been pleased to see them, for the first time he could remember, as he wished he could see them as a matter of course. It had affected him to see his parents in a way he never had or would again, because, as he had said, it was what he imagined marriage could be, not what he had seen it to be between them.

As she looked at the bed, she remembered the first bed they had shared, how they had lain side by side, after their first act of intimacy, she, shy and afraid of what had transpired, sore and waiting for some tender acknowledgment from him. He had turned to her. "How often have you done this?" he had said as he looked at her face. She hadn't been able to think, she had been so blindsided by the pain his question caused her, his intended insult and insensitivity tearing her up. All she had been able to say was, "What did you say?" "You heard me. How many times?" As she rose from the bed, tears of pain and indignation wetting her face, she could see the blood-stained sheets he still lay on. She was shocked by the amount of blood. It looked as though someone had been stabbed. What would the chambermaids think? Her mind whirled with hurt, indignation and sorrow that this act had been so wasted on him. Such a waste. She had offered herself with so much faith and love, believing he would take care of her, that he would appreciate the gift of herself that she had chosen to share with him. That he would love her more after this act that had joined them. But Nacho was, even then, Nacho, and his thoughts were wrapped up in himself. He had had no thought in his head of her feelings or needs. "I'm leaving. How dare you say such a thing to me? Who do you think I am? What do you think I am? Look at this room, look at me. How can you hurt me by saying what you just did without thinking of my feelings at all? I'm leaving."

"No, I didn't mean it like that. I was worried that's all, that I wasn't the first. I didn't mean to insult you." "Didn't mean to insult me? What are you talking about? I'm a good Greek girl from a good family. You know that you are insulting me." "No, no. I'm sorry. Don't be like that. I'm sorry. I love you. Don't be mad." She had given in, more needing of his affection than she was tied to her righteous anger, more needy of having her love affirmed rather than ready to deny it and walk away. Besides, it was done. She was committed. There was no going back. The bed was her witness. She couldn't undo what was done.

Before their wedding, they had argued for days as he insisted that they spend their first night in Vancouver before departing for Fiji in the morning. She knew of the Mexican custom of visiting the bride's family the morning after the wedding night and she hadn't wanted to do it his way. She hadn't wanted to have breakfast with her father and mother after spending her first night with her husband. "If you don't want to see your parents in the morning, then don't spend the night with me." "But if I don't spend the night with you, we won't be together for over a day before we get to Fiji, and we'll be exhausted by then." "No. If you don't want to see your parents in the morning, don't think of spending the night with me." After many angry words she had given in. The next morning, as they had driven up to her home, they parked behind a van full of his family and friends from Culiacan ready to go on a sight-seeing trip for the day. She had been mortified. She knew that everyone would be making jokes at her expense. It had been bad enough to have to face her parents, never mind a van full of people she didn't know very well. "Nacho, please go around the back and park in the garage." "No, why should I? Don't be silly. Who cares what they're going to say." "I care. I'm embarrassed! Could you please park around the back?" "No. I'm parking here and I'm getting out. Do what you want." He had parked the car and walked past the van, acknowledging the ribald jokes and comments with a laugh and a wave of his hand. She had sat in the car, upset, trying to decide what to do. She knew that everyone in the van would be turning to look at her. She looked foolish either way, whether she stayed in the car, or braved their comments and walked by. Finally, she got out and walked by his family and friends. They had been waiting for her, and it was just what she had expected as she looked down at the ground, walking by as quickly as possible with flushed cheeks and tears in her eyes. She had never forgiven him for what she saw as an act of humiliation, and he had never understood why it had bothered her so much.

Submit to the femininity that society demands of them.

She looked at the bed with the gently arched and beautifully upholstered headboard in peach fabric, the bed skirt complementing it with a gentle, ruffled hem and the bolster pillow covered in a romantic brocade of cherubs and ribbons, lace and organza. It was a king-sized bed and many times, over the years, Nacho would turn as he felt her spooning into his back in the dark, on his side of the bed, tapping his shoulder to let him know she was there.

Be his wife and would make home lovely to him.

Many times he had turned to her, joking that she left him no room. "Would you move? God, I'm going to fall off the bed!" He hadn't noticed, though she had, that months before Christmas she had begun to instinctively keep to her side of the bed, no longer seeking his warmth or his feet under the covers. Their roles had become reversed and it was now him, creeping to her side, seeking her out and leaving her no room by morning as he sought to reconnect with her. He had felt it and she had known, that it was too late, that whatever connection there had once been, it had been emotionally severed. It was a connection that she no longer needed or wanted.

Without the soul's union and commixture of intellectual delight, as it is rather a soiling than a fulfilling of marriage rights.

Two years ago, as she had begun to fight for her freedom and a life she found fulfilling and rewarding, he had become more difficult. He saw her education and her business, her time in Tucson, as threats that would take her away from him. In his mind they would bring her independence, and he hated them because of that. Even though she refused to concede defeat, the ongoing battle and the stress of all she was doing day in day out began to take their toll. She often lost faith that she would be able to fulfill her dreams, that her life would ever change, that she would ever have the relationship that she dreamed of, the life she wanted. She had waked in the dark, shuttered bedroom one Sunday, the down comforter pulled up to her chin, the soft pillows cradling her head in the gloom, and she had begun to cry. She had never cried like that before. She was afraid of the endless pain that tore through her mind because it felt infinite. It gripped her without relief as the tears became sobs, the sobs, an endless howl. She cried like a creature that had been tortured and left to die, its life worthless. Nacho had been awakened by her noise, but couldn't get her to speak. He tried to get her to tell him what was wrong. Only her mind screamed, "You're wrong. You're wrong. I want this pain to end. I don't want to live this life anymore. It's a living death. I'm dying, and there's nobody that cares." Eventually they weren't just sobs or cries, but the moans of a tortured, dying soul: a soul tortured beyond endurance, alive but in its death throes. That was how she had felt. She had no words, all she had was pure, raw, pain that stripped her of her life force down to an ember of burning, painful, essence. The pain was like a flaring blaze before its light was extinguished down to cold ash. A cold marrow. She had been so cold, but hadn't been able to say so. She had felt like her mind had lost the will to fight, the will to live. All she had been able to do was cry and lie there like a dead thing, only her moaning to prove she still had life.

I feel therefore I exist.

She had continued like that for hours, sobbing and sobbing as Nacho tried to lift her up, to talk to her, but she had been like a living rag doll. She hadn't been able to move, talk, or even turn her head. She hadn't been able to do anything except cry, the endless tears running down her face and into her hair, onto the bed, as she stared at the ceiling.

All day staring at the ceiling

Feeling like I'm headed for a breakdown.

Eventually, Nacho had called her counselor for advice, and the counselor had asked Nacho to hold the phone next to her ear. "You're going to be okay. I know that you feel like this will never end, but it will. It will pass. You need to eat something. Nacho is going to open the window and you're going to go outside today. That will help. Are you listening to me?" She sobbed in reply and could barely find the strength to say, "What's wrong with me?" "You're having a depression. You feel like you're going to die, but you won't. Not today, not from this. Hang in there. I'm going to call later to see how you're doing." She knew that he never lied to her. She believed him. Soon she was on her side, crying quietly, the sobs constant but less violent until at last she had none left. She had emptied herself.

> **The relief of speech is that it translates me into the universal.**

The mattress had been chosen and purchased by Nacho, an expensive, special-order mattress set he had indulged in because he loved to sleep as much as she didn't. As she looked at the bed, and remembered that horrible day, she felt disbelief that it could have been her. It seemed like a bad dream now. A nightmare. It had happened to her twice more, and the third time had passed fairly quickly, as she had determined to herself that she would never sink that low again. Nacho had left her to cry on the bed, walking out of the room, impatient and angry with what he saw to be crocodile tears. There would never be anything or anyone that would come that close to destroying her again. She had drawn her own line in the sand, a line that she would never cross again.

> **The mind is its' own place, and can make a Heav'n of Hell, and a Hell of Heav'n.**

It was April now and a few short months had passed since she had decided to divorce Nacho, but there was already a difference. As she looked at the bed, she realized that she had begun to read there again. She still didn't sleep much and probably never would, but the bed was no longer a place she endured, but a place where she rested, regrouped, dreamed and planned for the future.

> **The cool kindliness of sheets, that soon smooth away trouble.**

She had bought new sheets and bed coverings, bed clothes that she had purchased with pleasure and anticipation, the soft weft of the fabric lying under her cheek alone to soothe her as she healed and grew. She couldn't imagine ever having a big bed again. In her mind it gave the bed an importance that wasn't a part of her value system anymore, a value system that had evolved as she had grown in strength and in her definition of herself. She saw herself differently now, because now she knew what the bed was.

> **Man, the height of creation— the only creature with intellect, seeks intellectual love. Love which is less than intellectual is immicable to our unique nature and can only lead to suffering and unhappiness.**

Chapter TWELVE

The Bottles

Approaching the small, iron gate with its crossed bars and cast iron rosettes, she gazed up at the stone window set high in the wall. The space below the window was hung with two "dowry bags" reproduced from antique ones she had seen. They were made of linen, as the originals would have been, and marked with the date of her marriage minus one hundred years. Her maiden initials were marked on the front in faded sepia ink and numerated, two of a series, as the many bags belonging to a wellborn woman with substantial property would have been. She had chosen the numbers three and five to mark them. The number three represented her three children, the number five, the number they completed as a family. They were both odd and indivisible numbers, the number five one she had painfully divided into a fractured number. The number three was one that often repeated itself in her designs because she felt the connection it had to her children, as well as being a number that had the perfect aesthetic proportion. One professor had commented that there were some people who would subconsciously repeat a certain numeral throughout their designs, and she had discovered that she was one of them.

She had resisted including the wine cellar in the design of the house. Nacho had wanted a bar, and they had finally compromised by building the wine cellar. It was still incomplete. She had never put any effort or interest into its design, using it as a playroom for Stephanie until she outgrew her toys. She had gifted Nacho with the wine racks, the ornamental gate that locked off the racks of precious wine and had hung the "perfect" chandelier overhead with clusters of icy green grapes, scrolling vines and grape leaves. The resentment she felt towards every accoutrement bought for this room was disguised by their very attractiveness. In the corner of the room stood an antique Indian armoire that housed bottles of cognac, gin, whiskey, vodka and every other kind of hard liquor necessary to common hospitality. That was one of the few pieces in the house she would have happily given away.

Her parents had always had liquor available for their guests at home, and her father had educated her about every kind of liquor available as a teenager, often serving her wines of different bouquets and varieties and fancy cocktails to try so that she wouldn't be curiously drawn to the prohibited. She had only seen her father drink past his limit once, and had never forgotten the memory of him leaning out the window of her mother's new car as her mother drove home. In her childhood home, liquor had been a sign of hospitality, a beverage meant to complement a social gathering, but never used otherwise, except for the odd glass of wine or beer with dinner.

When she had begun to go out alone at the age of fifteen and had seen the attraction liquor had for her peers, it began to have a very different connotation. Everyone, it seemed, made it their mission to drink as much as they could as fast as they could. It had become a standard of social acceptance that was practically forced upon her as a condition of inclusion, a condition that she had not accepted. She was popular and sociable even though she didn't drink. The drinking repulsed and baffled her by the status it began to acquire, drunken binges recounted with pride amongst both the boys and her own girlfriends when they socialized on the weekends. She remembered one friend whose first sexual experience had been traumatic because her boyfriend had taken advantage of her when she was drunk, and then there was the party that had become a wake in a mansion on the North Shore of Vancouver when she was in grade eleven.

It had been the weekend when the private schools of the province had their best and brightest involved in debating and rugby competitions on the mainland and on Vancouver Island for two days. Everyone had planned to be at the party of the year, curious to see the home of the wealthy young man hosting it. The socially privileged youth from the different private schools in Vancouver planned to get together to party that Friday night and let off steam after their weeks of hard work. The evening became a surreal experience for everyone there. She remembered seeing teenage boys and girls crying and holding onto one another around the deck of the indoor swimming pool, young men walking around as though shell-shocked when the music was turned off and an announcement was made by a young man too young to be doing so, that four boys, four of St. George's best rugby players, had been in an accident, drunkenly crashing into the stone wall of the girls' school that night, killing one of them instantly and causing so much physical damage to the other three athletes that they were hospitalized for months. It was a savagely cruel and devastatingly conclusion to a "few hours of fun."

If you drink alcohol mindfully, you can see that it creates suffering. The intake of alcohol causes diseases to the body and the mind, and deaths on the road.

She had become increasingly wary of the attraction drinking had for her friends. She had finally been tempted to see what all the fuss was about and she had gotten drunk once, when she became legally of age, at a restaurant in Vancouver with a friend. That one time had been more than enough for her, the sensation of being legless and out of control was as completely unappealing to her as it was attractive to others.

She was intolerant of drinking in her friends, but after she met Nacho and came to know him better over the years, she saw that it was a part of him. Whenever they went out, it was inevitable that he would drink, and drink too much. She tolerated it, even as she voiced her discomfort and unhappiness with his behaviour.

She thought that he would change She didn't know what it meant. Not yet.

Once, after they had been married a few years, living in Culiacan, she and Nacho had left Thano and Nicholas at home with the housekeeper while they had gone out to a party at another couple's home. The home they had visited, as their own, was equipped with a "bar" that was a separate building attached to the house, where not just a cabinet or a room was used to house and promote the consumption of liquor, but a whole small building. Several of their friends had a "bar" in their homes, and it was one of the most desirable status symbols for wealthy males in that society. She had sat in the bar as the evening progressed, listening to the disco music playing, and had watched Nacho and the others consuming drink after drink, as she had done many times before, out of sync with a conversation that was becoming less and less coherent and more and more animated. She was tired of being bored and the odd one out, sick of being the only one sober and out of sorts because she wasn't drinking, and unwilling to subject herself in a sober frame of mind to the smell of him, the touch of him.

She had walked up to the bar and ordered a drink from the bartender, and when she had finished that one had ordered another, deciding that for once she wasn't going to be upset with the behaviour of her drunken husband when they got home, because she was going to be too drunk to notice.

Seizing his drinking cup as a defensive weapon.

It was when she had ordered her third drink that Nacho stopped drinking and came to sit beside her, and it was when she ordered her fourth and laughingly leaned on his arm that he had turned to her and in a savage undertone that no one else could hear, said to her, "That's enough!" his tone of voice had convinced her not to push her luck. She hadn't ordered another drink and they had soon gone home, their evening as spoiled as a bottle of sour wine, or the rancid smell of liquor she had smelt on his breath so many times. The many nights and days that his drinking had stolen and ruined for them both were lost, as were the nights and weekends she had spent alone with the children, Nacho wrapped in the arms of his bacchanalian muse.

She now knew that it was called alcoholism, and that, even though he hadn't been drunk in over a year, many of the reasons he behaved the way he did and treated her the way he did were because of the disease he couldn't or wouldn't address. It was an illness that would always be a part of him, as it was for so many others: an element of destruction that invaded lives and destroyed them in a socially accepted cancer of society. Even knowing that it would be abused, liquor was proffered ubiquitously, gifted at dinner parties and used as business barter in the bar and in the office, used as a social and sexual accessory, as a rite of passage for youth, as an outlet for inner sorrow and torment. She offered it in her home as well, and when she did, she was uncomfortable denying a guest the extra glass of wine or glass of tequila that they wouldn't deny themselves. Those who drank to excess revived too many painful memories of her life as it had been with Nacho and the coffee cup full of hot coffee flung at her head seemed as though it had happened yesterday. Memories of insults, harsh words and the many nights she had spent waiting for a key in the door at two, three, five, nine o'clock in the morning with anxiety and fear were scars that were still painfully sensitive.

She abhorred the wine cellar and the gentrification it created for a substance that had been the cause of so much destruction and pain. It seemed entirely appropriate that the terra cotta coloured Mexican tiles lead down, down to the lowest point in the house, down to the cool room closed off from the rest of the house by its studded leather door. It was the bowel of the house and should have been odiferous and foul to properly portray the disease that had seeped into their lives and pervaded that which had possessed the potential to be so good.

She had wanted to remove her sons from a world where drinking was encouraged and even thrust upon young males, as it was in Mexico. She had seen uncles encouraging their adolescent nephews to have a drink and then another and then another. So she had sent them to school in Canada, where life was cleaner and simpler. Thano's school on Vancouver Island had suspended him for drinking when he was fifteen. As one of the youngest players to participate in the rugby games that the school took them to play in Australia and Europe, he had drunk "*mano a mano*" with the older boys in a rite of passage that bonded them together. Those teachers of his who knew how to have a good time were especially esteemed by the boys, role models for what it took to enjoy life and let go, as were the adults who proudly endorsed their teenage son's inebriated toasts at their own adult parties. Nicholas had begun to drink as a teenager, as had

Stephanie, and they had often had words about how "anal" and intolerant they felt her attitude to be. It had been a memorable moment for them as a family that December two years before when she and Stephanie had come home early from the office Christmas party, and the boys had carried their father in the door at three in the morning. She had been beside herself that the boys saw this as acceptable, that they were being encouraged to see this as socially and parentally acceptable behaviour. She had been terrified that they would see it as a pattern to emulate. They had all been in the family room together as she sat in her chair by the fire and cried, insisting that Nacho acknowledge the damage he was doing. He eventually apologizing. The boys had been resentful, accusing her of overreacting. Stephanie, big eyed and quiet, had found it hard to believe this was being discussed openly by them as a family.

Thano got a D.U.I. at university, but reminded her that it wasn't a big deal; most of his friends had one. Nicholas followed a few years later, arrested for driving under the influence and behaving belligerently towards the arresting officer. Nacho took care of it both times, hiring good lawyers to beat the system and get the boys out of trouble, so that they wouldn't suffer any repercussions for their behaviour. Because drinking wasn't bad. Everybody did it except her. She was weird. She was odd. She was uptight and intolerant. She didn't understand that it was fun and the best way to socialize, network, make business deals, kick back, make friends, relax, get over a bad day, a tiring day, to celebrate a good day, a happy occasion.

She remembered how embarrassed she had been when they had been escorted out of the most exclusive club in Mallorca on their honeymoon, taken out the back door of the club into the alley and put into a taxi because Nacho was belligerent and drunk. They had originally missed their plane to Spain because he had attached himself to the bar at the Frankfurt airport. She remembered driving to the beach with him in Mexico on a hot, sunny Sunday with their two small boys, an ATV and a cooler full of beer for himself in the back of the truck. She remembered how she had refused to go to the family beach house in Mexico for Easter after fifteen years of watching the men get drunk day after day, year after year. Every year that beach vacation had meant an endless round of socializing from family to family, the adults drinking their way from house to house, boat to boat, the yachts sitting in the bay loud with laughter and music that carried over the water while the children played on the beach, in the sand and water, absorbing the message that this was the family way to holiday.

'Tis not the drinking that is to be blamed, but the excess.

She had offended everyone when she had not endorsed, ignored or denied what was going on. After they had moved back to Nogales and would visit Culiacan for family events, she would be a nervous wreck, anticipating, waiting for Nacho to come home at night after hitting the clubs with his friends or brothers after the day out with them. They had only been married a few years when Nacho had come home one night and, in an alcohol-driven rage, pushed her into the wall. She had gone to Chilo, her brother-in-law, the family patriarch now that their father was dead, and told him as Angela listened, that she needed him to intercede, that Nacho was becoming more and more aggressive and that he needed to talk to him. "Don't aggravate him," he told her. "Ignore him. It's because you provoke it. He doesn't fight with anyone else." Nacho had been furious and ashamed that anyone would know about their private life; he saw it as a betrayal of him and a betrayal of his family that she had spoken of things that should have been private. Secret things, that should have been sacred between husband and wife.

He had stopped drinking a couple of years ago, beginning to slow down after he had come home one night and seen the fear on her face as he walked up the steps in the atrium towards her. His wife was afraid of him. It had shocked him. He had finally recognized, even in his inebriated state, the consequences of his behaviour. He hadn't drunk excessively, just the occasional glass of wine for a couple of years now, but could still not accept that his illness was something that he would have to deal with all his life. She had. She had also understood that she couldn't help him if he didn't want to help himself. She couldn't fix this problem, she couldn't make him well, and she couldn't continue to live with it either. It had almost destroyed her. It had destroyed their marriage and damaged their family, especially the children to whom they had hoped to give the best of lives, the brightest of futures.

She looked through the gate, down the steps, but the door into the wine cellar wasn't visible; it was hidden around the corner. Like much of the destruction connected to the weakness it perpetuated, the devastation its contents had caused were internal, invisible, but especially invisible to those who chose not to see the power it had over their lives. The waves from the wine cellar seeped out the door and up the stairs, into the bodies and lives of those helpless to resist... "dancing like a Baccante over the... ruins of the lives it destroyed... 'till the seething grape-juice rose round... bare limbs in waves of purple bubbles... crawled in red foam" to convert the unsuspecting until it was too late.

For so many, it was a trap hard to resist or escape, which was why they had been lost to its siren's lure.

Chapter THIRTEEN

THE DOLL

Leaning over the bed in Stephanie's room, she straightened the pink mohair throw draped over the down comforter. As she stood up, she looked around the room she had created for her daughter. The bed was draped with pink curtains that were tied with bows onto the canopy, draped with the same fabric that covered the high, curved headboard and footboard. She had chosen a soft pink chintz with red rosebuds, small green leaves and pink confetti. It was such a girl's bed, as was the room such a girl's room with its green and pink palette and its collection of dolls on different chairs, tables and in the *faux marbre* cabinet next to her bed. Stephanie had never liked to play with dolls, and yet she had still collected them for her daughter. She hadn't wanted Stephanie to be the type of girl who played with dolls, and yet she bought them for her. Dolls encouraged girls to buy into a value system where women were meant to be both caretaker and nurturer. She wasn't even sure if that would be a fulfilling life for her daughter, but she collected the dolls for her anyway. Tradition was a powerful enemy to fight, even for someone who saw herself as a nonconformist.

> Custom, that unwritten law, By which the people keep even kings in awe.

There was a large picture hanging over the dark green velvet loveseat against the wall showing a group of young Victorian women furtively removing some books to read from a library case. The picture captured a moment in time, depicting a time when well brought up young women weren't supposed to fill their heads with thoughts that would overtax their less able minds. The young men they grew up with were supposed to be educated in order to lead productive lives; women didn't need to be productive, except in the procreative sense. It had been a message she wanted her daughter to be aware of. In many ways, in the world they lived in North America, at the beginning of yet another century, there were just as many rules and customs that seemed illogical, unfair and restricting to their gender, ones that were just as accepted, as that belief system had been then.

> Societies assume that certain customs are "Natural."

Above Stephanie's bed hung a framed print of a group of three women, women, again, of another era. The opulent bedroom in the picture indicated a life of privilege. They were gathered around the elaborate cradle of a newborn. It had seemed to her when she bought it a part of their own history, reminding her of her mother, Angela, and herself, as they had fussed over Stephanie, her first and only daughter, so cherished after such a complicated pregnancy. They had all been so happy for her, as she had been, to have a daughter for herself and a sister for her sons, so that they could grow up knowing the female perspective, and respecting the female perspective, having grown up with it. And she had a daughter for whom life held so much promise, a life that would be different, so much different than her own, different than her grandmother's, and different than women who lived in worlds, both geographical and cultural, where women's place would never be as societal equals to men's.

One sees that dead, vacant look steal sometimes over the rarest, finest of women's faces, in the very midst, it may be, of their warmest summer's day; and then one can only guess at the secret of intolerable solitude that lies hid beneath the delicate laces and brilliant smile.

The room was adorned with another picture hanging in front of the bed, this one of the Fairy Cottages in England, the cottages replicated and rebuilt in the San Juan Islands and painted by one of the nuns that taught her at the Convent. Nearby was placed a porcelain picture of a fairy, a bookcase for her own book collection, the picture of the girls determined to read what they liked, and dolls scattered and collected throughout her room. The obvious femininity of her daughter's environment was meant to be a celebration of her gender. She had gathered these things together for her, consciously and unconsciously, to influence her with her own beliefs, likes and history. Her value system was one that strove to enrich her life with knowledge and strength in her femininity, one that fought against the constraints imposed upon her gender, even as she wanted to celebrate every aspect of being female.

A child, more than all other gifts, Brings hope with it, and forward-looking thoughts.

Stephanie had sometimes rebelled against a mother who was as strong as she was, a mother who wasn't just her mother, but a woman striving to make her mark in the world as a person with a voice, asserting her independence. It was one of the relationships that most enriched her life, hers' with her daughter. She knew that Stephanie looked to her as a guide, and many times, when she felt that she couldn't go on, it was the thought of her daughter and setting a better precedent that kept her going.

The life we live is the lesson we teach.

Children learn what they live.

Every parent should remember that one day, their children will follow their example and not their advice.

She knew that Stephanie believed in her, and that made her even more determined to succeed and establish a new path. The new path was for both of them, a new path free of old traditions, the ones she and so many other women had been conditioned to follow, and she already saw in Stephanie so much that was new. She was the little girl who, at five, marched into school when two little boys looked up her skirt on the monkey bars and said that their behaviour was unacceptable. She was the one who said to her father, as her brothers never would, that the way he talked to her mother was not very nice. She was the child happy to play alone for hours, making costumes, reinventing herself, happy with who she was and confident in who she could be, constantly singing, because it was a part of her nature to sing the words of others, those and her own, creating a powerful human connection. That was her daughter.

The little child knows nothing of parental love, but only knows one face and one lap towards which it stretches its arms for refuge and nurture.

She reflected on the many young women she had met while back at university, women who were so bright and able, some in their twenties, some older, the women whom she called her friends, women who were smart, giving and kind, who had been so unconditionally supportive of her journey to fulfill her potential. Their company had enriched and sometimes challenged her to find her own way. There had been times when creating "the sisterhood" had been unexpectedly and inexplicably hard, yet, eventually, goodwill and progress had been made. She thought of her mother, the woman who had loved her unconditionally, even though she hadn't always been easy to love in the last few years as she fought to make her way independent of her mother's traditions. The traditions her mother didn't often question had trained her to put herself last, that had taught her that her own needs were unimportant and that she was meant to take care of her husband, children and grandchildren, never taking care of herself. Not if she were a good woman. And she thought of her sister, Angela, who had been the cause of so many of the decisions and choices she had made throughout her life, watching her older sister make her way, watching how her sister's choices and character constantly affected all of them in the family.

She walked over to the other side of the room and lifted up the doll on the bedside table next to Stephanie's bed. Angela had made it for her. It was a small teddy bear dressed in a Victorian outfit, sitting on an elaborate twig bench covered with flowers, berries and birds, holding a parasol. It was charming and so evocative of Angela, Angela and her love of Victoriana, her love of dolls and her love of the garden all manifest in one creation. She had made it for Stephanie, made it for her only sister's daughter, her only niece and her goddaughter.

Angela. When they were small, Angela had frightened her with stories of the evil Witch of the East after they had seen *The Wizard of Oz*, terrifying her until she crawled across the wood floor, through the dark hall, to her mother's bed. It was Angela who had convinced not just her, but all the neighborhood gang of under six-year-olds, to climb the rickety ladder in the musty, dark garage up into to the loft full of boxes and stacked up junk. Their mother had slammed the door of the garage shut in anger when she had finally gotten them all out, and, in slamming the garage door, where they weren't supposed to be playing, ripped out her fingernail on the loose doorknob. All of them had been traumatized to see the nail-less finger dripping blood, and they had all known that somehow Angela was the cause. Angela who had cried and made their mother cook home-made French fries, Greek-style in olive oil, so that her friend would stay and play. Angela, who had been the eldest and the ring leader every time the cousins were together, the one who organized and ordered everyone to light the bonfires at the beach in Osoyoos, filling big, old cardboard boxes full of newspaper and pushing them out into the still, dark, waters of the lake to watch them float out onto the liquid inkiness, the bright orange and gold flames dramatically bright in the endless darkness, reflected in the black, smooth, mirror of the glassy surface of the water. It was Angela who got them all to learn water skiing, to hike across town to the community beach, Angela who made her go snow skiing, to come home freezing cold and wet to the skin, smelling of wet wool. It was Angela who saved a little boy from drowning when she herself was only twelve, thereby becoming an even bigger hero to her sister and all her young cousins.

She had been the firstborn of both her mother's and her father's families and the cynosure of attention for two years, as a parade of adults flowed through her young parents home, because they were the only young Greeks with a house at the time. It had been Angela's role to be the family ringleader until they were teenagers. She had been the adored older sister her male cousins never had and, even now, when they were in their forties, they had a special relationship with her. She had been her hero as well, the older sister who was daring and seemingly unaffected by doing what she felt like instead of what she was supposed to do. It had bewildered and hurt her when Angela played the role of the older, independent sibling and didn't want her around. There had been many times that she went home alone after school because Angela didn't want her with her friends. In later years she had included her, when they were both adolescents, companions as they used the beaches and orchards of Osoyoos as their own backyard.

Their father had adored Angela as well. Angela had been his firstborn and, in many ways, the son he hadn't had. He was proud of the way she looked like him, that she bore his adored mother's name, that she teased and joked like him, could twist the truth like him, could shoot a gun like him, had green eyes like him, liked to eat like him, had strong legs and feet like him. Angela. Angela who had made friends with the young Mexican-Greek girl from Culiacan and had brought her to their home, befriended her, and begun a saga no one could have imagined. It was Angela who had gone to Mexico at the age of sixteen and come home laden with gifts, in love with her friend's older brother, and Angela who had been the reason two families met two years after that, the catalyst that brought the two worlds together. It was Angela who had married Chilo, Aspacia's brother, Nacho's brother, three years later, joining the families and moving from Vancouver to Mexico. It was Angela who had moved two thousand miles away from her family when her family was the most important thing in the world to her, leaving behind her identity, her cornerstone. She had taken herself away from her aunts, uncles, cousins, mother, father and sister, when her whole world had previously revolved around them. She tried to fit into the new world she found herself in, but the more she denied herself her roots, the more she pretended that she could deal with it, the more she was destroyed.

All happy families resemble one another, each unhappy family is unhappy in its own way.

Angela looked so strong, but was easily influenced by friends, adapting like a chameleon to the company she kept. Angela looked so strong, but she couldn't have her children naturally. She had four cesareans, the first one an emergency that almost cost her and her baby their lives. Angela looked so strong, but she was diagnosed with lupus when she was thirty. Angela looked so strong but was as hooked on cigarettes as any junkie on dope, coughing, hacking for hours as the nicotine stuck in her lungs. Angela looked so strong, but the strain of living a life that was foreign to her was compensated for with food, depression and denial. Angela looked so strong, nobody believed that she couldn't do it all until she walked out the door of her house in Culiacan and left her home, her possessions, her children and her husband behind. A plane ticket back to Vancouver in her hand, she was done with pretending to herself and everyone else that she was strong enough to survive being away from her life blood, her family, her roots. In many ways she had a code that was the same as her husband's family. Blood, blood, blood. She too had confused the importance of the family she had created with the family that she came from. It was more important for her children to be with their cousins than to be a family in and of themselves. But that was all right. In the world of Culiacan, that was the way it was supposed to be. Cousins were supposed to be like siblings, and anyone who did not buy into that value system was disloyal, a betrayer. Bad. Angela understood their value system because it was her own as well. She didn't question it, she didn't fight it, and she didn't deny it. She accepted it and wanted it for her sister as well, but by accepting it, she had to understand in the back of her mind that no matter how much time passed, no matter how well she adapted, no matter how well she adopted their traditions, spoke their language, ate their food, lived in their country, she would never, ever, be one of them. There was nothing she could do to make herself part of the family, because she would never be of their blood. She would always be an outsider, a foreigner, a Greek-Gringa.

When Angela had left Chilo, the reactions of Nacho's family to the one sister were a sure indication of what was coming her way as she gauged their relationship to her as well. They professed to love her, but every time they knew of a situation where Nacho had treated her badly, they had turned the other cheek. Every time they had treated her badly, Nacho had been unsupportive, choosing his siblings and mother over her. She had been wrenched at the manner in which Angela had left her four children. Her youngest son, Michael, had been twelve at the time. Angela had left her children when her eldest son was psychologically fragile, her daughter involved with an abysmal boyfriend and her middle son desperately needy of attention and love. Her children had all needed her, and she had left. It had taken another year before she could understand the depths of Angela's depression, understand that it had been eroding her for years and years. She didn't know if she would ever forgive her for leaving Chilo just as she had decided to leave Nacho. Angela had listened to her for a year; she had stayed with her in Vancouver that summer of 2000 at their parent's, she had heard every step of her process in deciding whether her marriage could be salvaged or not, then she had left. She had known that she was planning to leave Nacho, she had heard her plans, listened to her agonize and then bolted the same day she had decided to separate, leaving her sister to pick up the pieces her frantic exit had caused.

She felt shipwrecked. Swimming, swimming; uncertain of her position but determined to survive.

That was how it had felt. Angela had jumped ship and sacrificed her sister to save herself. Her loving, older sister had abandoned her when she knew how bad it was for her, to save herself. The summer of 2001 that Angela had left Chilo was a milestone in her blood family, as well as in her relationship with Nacho.

That year, the year she had been going to separate from Nacho, was symbiotically tied to that moment in time in Osoyoos when they were young, she and Angela alone with their dad upstairs at the restaurant. They had been alone with their father in the banquet room with the seamless windows providing a one hundred and eighty degree view of the orchards, town and lake. The room was stripped bare after some event or another, chairs and boxes stacked to the sides of the room on the linoleum floor. Angela had done something to upset their father; she didn't remember what it had been, except that their father had been unusually angry with Angela, upset in a way that had him in one of his rages, shouting at her while she denied any wrongdoing. She had watched the two of them as they argued, a spectator, until her father undid his belt and began to pull it out of the loops of his pants. Angela was going to get it. He was really mad. Angela had seen the look of anger on her father's face and known that there was not going to be any way to talk herself out of the situation. She had been caught and her father was holding her accountable. She had raced across the room even as her father called after her, leaping over the crates of glass soda bottles with the ease of a hurdle jumper, racing down the stairs before he could punish her for her misdeed. Their father had been apoplectic. Belt in hand, he had turned to her, his youngest daughter, grabbed her by the shoulder, turned her around, and smacked her with the belt. She had never forgotten it. He had never hit her before. It had seemed like a metaphor for her relationship with her older sister ever since. Angela made a mess; her sister had to deal with it. Worse yet, she was not to create any trouble, because Angela always seemed to create more than enough for everyone.

Angela had left her husband, had left her children— and she had stayed. If Angela couldn't make it work, she had to. If Angela made a mess of her life, she wouldn't, couldn't. She wasn't going to cause anyone any trouble. Angela did that, not her. Angela. Angela who was sick, who constantly battled her weight, her emotions, who was always up, who was always the life of the party, who never tired of putting others first, who never complained about her fevers from the lupus, from the aches and pains the disease caused, the one who never said that the disfigurement from the illness destroyed her self esteem, who never spoke of the lupus except to deny that it affected her or that she even had it. Angela. Her mother's favorite topic of conversation as she worried about her health, her lack of foresight, her untidy habits, the lack of her own home, her troubled grandchildren, her lack of thrift, her isolation in Mexico, her dependence on the people who weren't her family. Angela, Angela, Angela.

Her nieces and nephews adored her. She was the aunt who was the most fun, the most giving, and the one who always had something interesting to talk about, something fun to joke about. Her husband's family and all the community in Culiacan had adopted this Canadian-Greek girl as though she were one of their own, but she wasn't. Her husband Chilo was, and she had left because she didn't belong there.

> **People only revolt when they have been badly treated.**

Her own children loved their aunt Angela as well, because in the years they were small, she was happy to let them live off of pizza, Chinese take-out and watch any videos they wanted day after day after day, until they begged for some order in their lives again. After a couple of weeks of Aunt Angela, their own home and routine had a new appeal. When their favorite aunt had left their cousins to go to live in Vancouver again, there had been a lot of anger and pain. Whenever they went to Vancouver now, she was a part of the routine that previously had meant solely being with their grandmother and grandfather. They watched her life change and they watched their grandparent's lives change. It seemed like the inevitable reaction now, everyone's, when she told them she was going to divorce Nacho. "Why are you doing what she did? Why both of you?" She had been, and was, so resentful that she wasn't allowed the dignity of dissolving her own marriage of twenty-three years without it being affected by Angela and her actions again.

She had to reiterate over and over that her marriage and Nacho's had its own issues, its own problems, while everyone tried to make sense of the situation as reflecting a foursome. They weren't a foursome, they were two twosomes, two sisters married to two brothers whose marriages had been painfully dysfunctional, but each with their own set of dynamics. The fact that they were two sisters from another country married to two brothers was too unique not to dominate the other facts though, to the point that additional facts weren't even pertinent as far as others were concerned. They had told the same story endlessly over the years. "How did you meet?" And the story that followed never failed to elicit, "Oh my God, what a story, two sisters married to two brothers, from Mexico, from Canada, Greeks, who would have thought? Do your children look alike?" And of course they and everyone else expected them to be so similar as to be identical in every way, individually and as families, but just like any family, they had their idiosyncrasies and their similarities. The effect of one marriage upon the other had been unanticipated by any of them, and none of them had been prepared to deal with the aftermath as one marriage rebounded off of the other.

The first time Nacho had pushed her into the wall, angry and drunk, she had turned to Angela and Chilo for help. She had gone to their house the next morning as Nacho slept off his late night at the bar, and she remembered it as though it were yesterday. Their expressions. Neither of them wanted to hear what they were hearing, much less deal with it. "Nacho pushed me into the wall, hard, last night. He didn't slap me, he didn't hit me, but nobody pushes me around. He was trying to intimidate me. It will not happen again. You need to talk to him. You're his older brother and you're the only one he'll listen to." "I'll talk to him," Chilo said. "But you must have done something to provoke him. He doesn't behave like that with anyone else. Don't bother him, don't talk to him, don't do anything when he comes home after he's been out drinking."

Why man makes a beast of himself through drunkenness.

Angela had been silent, hadn't said a word either in support, affinity or criticism. She had expected Chilo to be true to his word and speak to his brother, but she knew that he never had. To the contrary, by refusing to acknowledge what his brother had done and by refusing to address it, by continuing to take his brother to bars himself, he was declaring her confession and search for help to be invalid. There was nothing wrong with his brother; she was the problem. "Don't talk to him when he comes home drunk, don't aggravate him, and don't provoke him. He doesn't fight with other people. You must be doing something." She remembered when Nacho had come home early in the morning from a late night out with his friends. He had been sleeping when she had gathered up his smoky clothes to put them in the wash. Thano had been playing by her feet, not yet walking well, when she emptied the pockets of Nacho's jeans and had taken out a package from his pocket. She had never seen a condom before, and it had taken her a second to digest what she was looking at. Thano had been asleep in his crib when she had confronted Nacho with the condom in her hand. "What are you doing with one of these in your pocket?" *"Coma cres Mijita?* Do you really think that with a woman like you to come home to, that I would even look at anybody else? You can't be serious. It was just a prank that one of my friends played on me. It doesn't mean anything." She had called Angela, distraught, crying. She explained what had happened. "Don't take it so seriously. His friends probably did play a joke on him. I mean, why would he do something like that? Don't worry about it." She remembered showering, Thano playing by her feet in the spraying water, as she tried to decide what to do. If she left, Thano wouldn't have a father to raise him. What if she was wrong? What if it was a prank one of his friends had pulled? What if her suspicions were unfounded? She didn't really have any proof.

As in thought, no image of one's own body figures at all in intuition.

She decided to stay, but her conversation with Angela had been a large part of that. Angela hadn't supported her suspicions, but had rather denied them. Angela had wanted her to stay too.

Twenty-two years later, after Angela had left Chilo, she had spent night after night listening to Chilo as he tried to come to terms with Angela's abandonment. It had been an odd position to be in, to be both the sister-in-law to her husband's brother and the sister to the ex-wife as well. Society, family, nieces and nephews had all had a hard time defining where she fit in the picture, and had finally almost accepted her because she was a "good" woman who had stayed. Accepted her until the strain of avoiding conversations that included her sister in them had become too complicated and they decided to avoid her. By then, she too was tired of dealing with any of it and pretty much avoided anyone from that world as well. The stress of living in the never-never land between the two families had become tremendously difficult. Then Angela decided that she wanted to be with her children in Culiacan for that first Christmas. The whole family was upset and confused. Women in Culiacan "never" divorced, and if they left, they didn't come back. No one knew how to deal with the situation with any grace and she, the sister, muddied the situation even more. She was the sister of the woman who had left, which made her bad, but she was also the wife who had decided to stay, so that made her good. Or did it? Which one was she? She wasn't supportive of Angela leaving, because she had left her children as well, but she didn't believe that she should have stayed with Chilo either. Everything was supposed to be clear; judgments were to be made, sides taken, relationships defined. This was a situation that defied clarity.

She decided that the best solution would be if their family went to Culiacan for Christmas as well. They hadn't spent Christmas there for years. She hadn't wanted to and had suggested to Nacho that perhaps the stress of the situation would be mitigated for his mother if she were kept occupied with their family as house guests. Meanwhile, Angela would be staying in her home with her children and Chilo, a situation that no one was comfortable with. In the past, whenever they were in Culiacan, she and the children had spent all of their time at Angela's house; the children were all almost the same ages as their cousins and had spent all their lives in one another's' company. When they got to Culiacan though, the tension was palpable. Wherever they went, loyalties were challenged, opinions suppressed and convictions voiced. Everyone's feelings were in a heightened state of alert.

As usual, the day after they arrived they went to Angela's house, Angela's house where Angela was no longer the woman of the house. She had left seven months earlier and now resented the fact that decisions had been made and her home reorganized without her. It didn't seem as though she knew what she wanted. She had left Culiacan, but here she was in Culiacan. She had left Chilo, but she was here to see if Chilo still wanted her, if something could be worked out. She and Angela had not communicated for months. She still couldn't get over the fact that Angela had left the same day she had been ready to leave Nacho, and she hadn't been able to deal with the fact that she had left all of her children behind and moved two thousand miles away, leaving their care and attention in the hands of their father, who, until now, had left all that to Angela. He had to try to catch up quickly to the responsibilities of being a "single" father and had done as best as could be expected on some fronts, just as he had fallen abysmally short on others.

For the last few months Angela had been trying to build up a business that she had already established, that of liaison, taking Mexican students to Vancouver in a home stay program. It had seemed like a safe and innocuous way to spend time together while in Culiacan, for her to help Angela with the text of her web-site. Their interaction was tense. They tried to make conversation as their children hung out. The kids seemed determined to ignore what was going on between their mothers and behave as though the past few months and this visit were the same as though nothing had happened. They were all playing games. Nobody really believed it, but it was what they were hanging on to, to pretend that they did.

Pretense and reality.

When she walked into Angela's house that first morning, she found Angela on the computer. She had been told by several family members, Angela's children and by Chilo, that Angela was addicted to the computer, that she would chat on it for hours at a time, oblivious to what was going on around her. Angela knew that she knew. "Good morning," she said as she sat down in a chair next to her. Angela looked upset. "What are you doing?" "Nothing." "Who are you talking to?" "A friend I've made through my backgammon club in Cypress. Why?" The tone sounded defensive. A tone she had heard often in conversations with her sister. This was not going to be a good day. "You sound upset." "Well, the girls are going to go because it's Christmas Eve. I've been cooking all morning for the dinner tonight and this woman has to go. Chilo didn't give this new housekeeper her money today, and her son has leukemia, and she doesn't have any money to pay the doctors today." "Well, Angela, I'm sure he forgot. I don't think it was intentional on his part." "It's the same. He's so caught up in what he's doing at the office; he forgets that other people have needs too." "There's nothing you can do about it. Why get so involved? He hired her, he'll deal with it. You're going to be gone in a few days and you have enough to deal with without worrying about her too." "God, I hate it when you do that! You think that you have all the answers. Has it ever occurred to you that you don't?" She left the room and went to look for the boys. They were her ride; they had the keys to the car. "Where are your brothers, Stephanie?" "I don't know. They went out." She felt panicky. "Do you want to walk down to the Obregon? We can go get some ice cream." Stephanie looked at her as though she had lost her mind. Without thinking about it, she knew that people of a certain class did not walk in Mexico. What was wrong with her? "I don't want ice cream." "Let's go across the street, then to the corner store." "What's up with you, Mom? I don't want to go anywhere. I just want to stay here and watch TV with Michael." She felt as though the walls were closing in on her, disaster looming over her shoulder.

She walked into the kitchen and hitched herself up onto the counter as Angela entered from the other door. Angela's face was tight with anger. She sat on her hands and looked at the floor as Angela began to furiously wash dishes in the sink. "Isn't the housekeeper going to do that?" "She left. I told her to go so she could deal with the doctors." "So. How has it being going? Has it been okay?" "Okay? How can it be okay? We haven't seen each other for four months and he comes home late at night so we haven't been able to talk." "Do you want to talk to him? I thought that you didn't want to see him or talk to him anymore. That's why you left." "I left because I couldn't talk to him. That's why. We couldn't communicate." "Well, he told me that he still loves you, that he misses you. He's been calling me pretty often to tell me that." "Well, he's calling the wrong person. Why doesn't he tell me? He's such a chicken shit." "You mean that you want to come back?" She was floored. "Why do you think I'm here?" "I don't know, Angela! If you don't know what you want, how am I supposed to?"

She jumped off the counter as she finished her sentence. "I hate your air of superiority! You have the answer for everything. I couldn't have a worse enemy than my own sister. You! My sister." And with that she slapped her in the face. Hard. Then she continued. She hit her in the shoulder, on the arm, and her bracelet broke, beads scattering on the floor. She hit her on the hip. "What are you doing? Stop it! Angela!" "Get out of my house! Get out of my house, and don't you ever come back. Get out!" she screamed. Michael came bursting through the swinging door and held on to his mother, holding her arms against her. *"Mama! Mama! Que estas haciendo? Mama!"* She couldn't even think straight. She bent shaking to collect the beads off the floor. She had to do something while she tried to compose herself.

> He who makes a beast of himself—gets rid of the pain of being a man.

She picked up all the beads, got her purse from the kitchen chair and said, "I have to go now." She could hardly make the words come out. Angela was crying, Michael still holding onto her, but more as an embrace. Shaking, she walked through the swinging door. Stephanie was sitting as though carved from stone on the sofa, her eyes glued to the television. "Stephanie, I have to go. Are you coming?" "No. I'm staying here with Michael." Another wave of pain hit her, this one internal. Stephanie didn't want to be involved. It was as though she were saying to her face, "Don't involve me. Don't make me take sides. Don't make me take your side. If I stay, I haven't taken a side. Go away so I don't have to think about it. If I don't see you, it didn't happen." She looked at her daughter and she understood. She felt as though her heart would burst. "Okay. Steph. I'm leaving now." Stephanie just nodded.

She walked out of her sister's house, the house that wasn't where her sister lived anymore, and opened the front door of the house, the door she didn't know if she would ever open again, and stepped out into the hot, humid air as she began to sob. She was walking, walking, walking, without knowing where to go, blindly putting one foot in front of the other just to keep moving. The scene she had just left kept replaying itself in her head as she kept moving down the dirty sidewalks, her shoulders heaving with her tears, her hand swelling as she walked. Angela. Angela. Angela. She couldn't digest it. It had been Angela.

She remembered that the first time they had been separated was that summer when Angela had traveled down to Culiacan at the age of sixteen. She had been thirteen and had missed her older sister badly. She had written her a little note and given it to her upon her return, saying how she had missed her, loved her. Angela had read it and tossed it aside as she unpacked her suitcases, her expression dreamy, her head full of romance, images of Chilo and the exotic country she had just traveled from. No little sister could compete with that, and she had known then that their relationship was forever changed; that her sister was no longer hers. That 24th of December, 2001 was the tragic outcome of what began that summer so many years before.

As she set the beautiful doll back on the table, she pushed away the sadness. She couldn't let it bother her anymore. She and her children, they all pretended that it had just gone away, but she still couldn't be near Angela. She couldn't physically be near her anymore. She would greet her politely with a kiss to the cheek when she was in Vancouver, but being in each other's company was strained, different. She had never thought that she was a person to hold a grudge, and she didn't feel it was that. It just hurt too much. Angela had asked her therapist to call her a couple of months later and tell her how upset she was by what had happened. That had made it worse, and they had never really discussed it again. The blow to her hand had taken months to heal. She suffered periodically from tendonitis now, from writing on the computer for school, and the blow had ruptured the sheath to her tendon. The swelling of her hand, the pain, had gone away months later, when she could finally deal with what had happened, the outward injury such a blatant manifestation of the inward trauma. The injury was still there, somewhere, though, as was the doll, a memory of the sister she had once had. Angela.

That which purifies us is trial and trial is by what is contrary.

Chapter FOURTEEN

The Pillows

She walked through the stone-coping between the dining room and the living room and sat down on one of the pair of coffee and cream sofas she had designed. With huge suede pillows padding the back, fringes of fresh green, camel and cream, they framed the smaller pillows in the middle of each sofa like the guardians of royalty. The two smaller pillows were hand embroidered and had taken months to complete, the intricate pattern of the heads of the male and female pugs dressed for court so complex and detailed that they had needed the skills of a master embroiderer to execute them. The master embroiderer had been her mother. The pillows of the elegant pug couple sat on the paired sofas, in the room full of coupled furnishings. The furnishings, pairings, that were metaphors of how she had identified herself, as had her mother, clearly stating that she and her mother's identity for so many years were that of one-half of a couple. A wife.

Her mother had been so proud that her daughter had married well, a man at least half Greek, a man who could provide her daughter with every material object her heart desired, a man who would understand their traditions and not scorn them as foreigners, a man that would respect his wife's important role as a mother, if not a wife. That was part of the Greek tradition, as well as the Mexican. Women in Greece tended their males, they cooked for them, they cleaned up after them, they served them, and they were second-class citizens to them. The men ruled the home, the men gave the orders, the men made the important decisions, the men had financial control, the men defined themselves through their work, and their wives defined themselves as wives and mothers. If the women worked, it was just work, not their purpose in life, as it was their husbands.

> I don't know any business you have to think about at all. Thinking does not become a young woman.

Their work didn't count, wasn't acknowledged or usually appreciated. That's what women were supposed to do. But the men really worked, really got tired, and came home to rest while their wives continued with children, dinner and cleaning.

Six months after she had decided to divorce, her parents still couldn't accept her decision; they were ashamed and embarrassed to acknowledge to their friends and family what they saw as a failure in all of their lives. They had portrayed her to all as having the perfect life. They had wanted to believe that she had the life they had dreamed of for her. As immigrants who had worked so hard to achieve the material wealth that had been an unattainable dream in Greece, they believed that material wealth had to equate with happiness. They had turned a blind eye to all the signs and symptoms of her pain and unhappiness, in part because the men and the women they knew all lived in a constant battle of the sexes.

One morning, after her decision to divorce became an ongoing discussion between her parents and herself, she had defied her mother, saying, "You get up in the morning and the rest of the day your day revolves around whether Daddy had enough rest or not, whether he ate or not, whether he enjoyed his food or not, if what he ate bothered his stomach or not, if he's in a good mood or not. Well, I refuse to live that way. I deny your legacy. I deny your choice. It is not mine. My life's purpose is not going to revolve around Nacho and his wants and needs, his anger and his control. I choose differently. That part of my life is over."

> **We must try to recognize what in our accepted tradition is damaging to our fate and dignity— and shape our lives accordingly.**

She remembered entering her mother's bedroom in Vancouver. Time after time, whenever she would make a visit, her mother would be using yet another skein of wool or silk as the project of the two pillows progressed. Her mother would show off her handiwork proudly, recounting her efforts to discern the pattern of the lace collar on the female's ruff or the shadows on the face of the male, inviting her acknowledgment and praise, as she did every time she cooked a meal, got dressed or did something in the house. She wanted the validation her husband never gave her for fifty years, or her family before that, for the first twenty. She had been a woman in post-World War II Greece, the first born of her siblings and, unfortunately, a female.

Her mother hadn't often recounted her personal history as a woman raised in that era, and so it seemed as though she preferred to forget those years and those memories, erase them. She wasn't anxious to return to Greece as often as other Greek immigrants, especially family members close to them, and didn't romanticize the past and her heritage as her husband did. She preferred to forget it, as though it had never happened. She hadn't been as happy in Greece as she was in Canada. She had adopted her new homeland with a fervent patriotism shared by none of their fellow Greek family and friends. They all spoke of and adhered to their Greek heritage with unreasonable tenacity, just as her mother did to her new, Canadian one. All she had heard from her mother over the years was that she had wanted to leave Greece. Post-World War II Greece had no opportunities for anyone, especially for a woman. In such a patriarchal society, what was expected of her was that she cook, clean, marry, have children and help with the farming in a village where everyone was a farmer. Her mother had had to fight for her right to an education, because her brother, although younger, was the boy, and so more deserving of the financial sacrifice an education would incur; she was a useless girl who would only waste it on having babies.

> Women... do not always produce children... but their proper purpose is to produce them.

She had fought for and earned the right to go to school and be taught history, math, Latin, gymnastics. The few stories she had heard from her mother over the years were of her school years in Tripolis. She had been taught to embroider at school, as all well brought up girls were, learning the art proficiently, but she didn't know how to cook or sew. She had taught herself those other important housewifely skills after immigrating to Canada at the age of eighteen. She had been brought to Canada by her father's brother and his Canadian wife, a childless couple in their fifties who had sent money from Canada to pay for her schooling in Greece as well. They had treated her as a daughter, but it was especially Lydia, her great-aunt by marriage, who had a great impact on her. Her mother had seen for the first time a woman as equal, superior to her spouse in business, in intellect, in character and in height.

> Do you not know I am a woman? When I think, I must speak.

Lydia Arsens was campaigning for provincial election when her mother had arrived from Greece at the age of eighteen. She had been a tall, blonde woman of German descent from the Canadian prairies. She had passionately advocated the value of education even before she arrived in British Columbia. A schoolteacher by profession, she was extremely bright, well educated, and a woman of high integrity. She was also a wonderful cook, and an excellent homemaker, attributes often referred to in the political press releases over the years. They also commented on her ability to dress well and her inability to see when she was wrong. Tall, she towered over her short, dark, uneducated Greek husband in so many ways that what their young niece saw was a strong willed couple hopelessly mismatched, bound together for life in a battle for supremacy.

Lydia had been unfortunately ahead of her time. She was one of the first women to be elected to government in Canada in the nineteen-fifties and never really adapted to the political arena, unwilling to compromise her values and opinions to be politically correct. She had advocated recycling and promoted the supreme value of education, parental involvement in education and a natural, healthy life style with foods free from pesticides and herbicides at a time when the use of the new chemicals were the golden key to agricultural success. She was seen as a quack. She was the only woman at the time with a seat in the legislature of British Columbia, but despite that great achievement, her Achilles heel was that she was too straightforward, too intelligent, and adamant, offensively so, becoming the favorite target of the local newspaper editors when she objected to the paragraphs devoted to her wardrobe and her homemaking skills, even as her political opinions were satirized and belittled.

> **If liberty means anything at all, it means the right to tell people what they do not want to hear.**

The young woman from Greece, living in their home, watched and learned. She saw that a woman could be educated and influential, but that her gender would always compromise her power and intelligence. At the end of the day, she would be seen as a wife and a woman, not an equal. The second sex. It was a message the young woman from Greece passed on to her daughter as well, just as her mother and her great aunt had passed it on to her.

Her mother had made the curtains for their family's home when they couldn't afford to buy them, slipcovers for the sofas, clothes for herself and her little girls. She had learned to cook after her husband and his two brother's insatiable appetites had made it a necessary skill to supply the full household the young couple found themselves heading. The obligations placed upon her every day to satisfy the young men's need for food caused many tears and fights in their home. Her in-laws came from Greece, and, as with many immigrant families, it was her duty, as wife, to look after them as well. They demanded respect and expected to be waited on. She had her two small girls to look after and her own sister had come from Greece to live with them and help out until she got on her feet. It was a full house. She had left poverty and limitations in Greece to have every opportunity given to her, but she had rejected the opportunities her aunt and uncle offered her, denying herself an affluent home in Victoria with her "adoptive" parents to marry for love. She married an impoverished young Greek man with only a certificate from business school in Greece to his name. She had married against her aunt's and uncle's wishes, never admitting to herself or anyone else, that life would have been very different had she not felt with her heart and thought with her head. Her married life began with romance and dreams and endured years of arguments, deprecation and belittlement. She and her husband competed fiercely, as she was determined to be respected and acknowledged, while he was equally determined to be the unchallenged head of the house. It was a no-win situation that their two little girls grew up immersed in. They saw marriage as combat, not a partnership; they saw marriage as a battle of the sexes, unrelenting and unequal. They saw that the wife had a role to play, as did the husband, and when the lines were crossed it was all-out war with victory for none.

The marital legacy they gave her sister and herself was unintentional, just as the one Nacho absorbed in his family was as well. Nobody then thought to challenge the belief system, as they still didn't in Mexico, that the wives and daughters were meant to serve the men their food first, running to attend to the males, to be separate, socially segregated into gendered groups and gendered occupations. These things nobody challenged, never mind questioned, because they didn't even see them.

Many people make up their minds — even about important issues — on the basis of very little information except what society tells them is normal.

Mexico, the world she had entered when she married Nacho, was the world of the wealthy, a world of the privileged few in a country of immense social dichotomy. In the world of privilege, women spent hours a week on their appearance, not their personal growth.

Females are especially burdened by the attention they receive for their pleasing appearance.

Men controlled the finances, rules and regulations of the house, and roamed about freely, just as the women were expected to stay in a domestic arena where they could be controlled, watched over, safeguarded, "jailed." The women had household help: cooks, chauffeurs, nannies, until they became dependent upon a staff of people to cater to them and pamper them, remaining the "defenseless female" until their deaths, their most important contribution, procreation. Few did social work, in spite of the overwhelming need, perhaps because the vast quantity of underprivileged and poor intimidated them as much, if not more than, taking the initiative to promote social change in a country where social change had been dormant since the Mexican Revolution. In Culiacan, civic and social responsibility were asleep, or worse yet, dead.

She had lived in Mexico, in Culiacan, for five years, and, in retrospect, had never heard of a culture that celebrated mother's day on an equal scale. The most impoverished found time off to celebrate the "female role in procreation," though to couch it in such terms would certainly be culturally offensive and somehow sacrilegious. Perhaps because in their world the role of mother was so indelibly linked with the Catholic image of Mary; the Catholic and the pagan had become inextricably entwined. In Mexico it was unclear to most which was human and which was sacred. One sociologist's analysis suggested that in the Mexican culture, love for women was from the waist up and for the men, from the waist down. The last few years in Culiacan had seen a plethora of privileged young women going fat bellied to the altar as they fought to break through archaic sexual standards, standards that confined them to celibacy or marriage. Premarital sex almost inevitably ended in pregnancy, as the social constraints condemned those who thought to use contraception as promiscuous. In that world it meant that the young woman had premeditated the sexual act, which made it far worse in their minds than a young woman who became pregnant through God's will, by accident, or because she was in love with the boy and didn't think of the consequences. Pregnancy and shotgun weddings were preferred to contraception and safe, premarital relationships.

The poor were worse off. Woman after woman became pregnant time after time as they sought to keep a mate by trying to create a moral obligation to themselves through the man's offspring. They were culturally conditioned to believe that progeny would tie a man to a woman as long as she continued to impregnate herself, feeding his need to affirm his virility. No such act of conscience occurred, of course, and the cultural norm was to see a woman with children begat by several men trying to raise the children as a single mother. They rarely married, though constantly repartnered. Amongst the wealthy as well, manliness was determined by an arcane value system that enabled and socially condoned men's sexual promiscuity without consequence. Those who were American born, with a different, "American" value system, would recount tales of the local "rich and famous" who could be found supporting the whore houses and taking to mistress pretty bank clerks who might be lucky enough to have a house and financial support from a wealthy patron. It was common knowledge that the well-to-do often sired several illegitimate families. Even amongst Nacho's family, the women whispered tales of the reported liaisons and questionable illegitimate offspring amongst them. The "real" women were considered to be those who would confront the whore/mistress and, being the more womanly victor, keep her husband by her side. Real women kept their men; the pathetic ones lost them to the whores. None of them seemed to understand the American/Canadian perspective that a whoring spouse was undesirable, perhaps because the American/Canadians had yet to understand that a woman in Mexico without a man was essentially defenseless and penniless unless she had her own family's wealth to support her.

There were no divorce settlements in Mexico, there was no spousal maintenance; the woman always lost and lost badly if she chose to leave a bad relationship. It wasn't just a question of Catholicism, if was the powerful facts of economics. She was on the street, and in Mexico the street was what it was in pre-industrial society in the rest of the Western world, a society without social benefits, without shelters, without equal rights laws, without social justice. It was a world socially two hundred years behind the rest of North America, and the differences would not be evened out for several generations, if ever.

Women were still expected to be virginally pure and the men sexually promiscuous. Women were still expected to stay home while the men caroused in bars and whorehouses until the early hours of the morning. This was the world she had to adapt to when she moved to Mexico at the age of twenty, coming straight from Vancouver, and she was given no leeway for cultural differences. The only way that Nacho and his family would tolerate her was if she adopted their customs unconditionally. Otherwise she was immoral and depraved, a contaminated "american" with a small "a." She and her sister were "lucky" that their Greek heritage saved them from being considered promiscuous Canadians and, in consequence, unsuitable marriage material.

Down on your knees
And thank heaven,
fasting, for a good
man's love.

She remembered once driving in Culiacan with some of Nacho's small nieces in the car and speaking in English. A small girl in the car had said in surprise, *"Es gringa, tu tia?"* The quick response was then, as it had been for Nacho many times, *"No, es Griega,"* clarifying the cultural distinction between themselves and other Americans and "saving" them from social stigma by virtue of their desirable European descent. The connotation, of course, being that Greeks had the same superior value system as Mexicans. In the eyes of the Mexicans, Americans didn't respect hearth and home or family and had a value system that was immoral and depraved, degenerate. They were the cause of the fall of Western civilization, but that didn't stop the Mexicans from buying their goods and sending their children to American schools to learn English. The parents imposed one inviolable condition on their children when they ventured abroad, and that was that they not mix with or get too close to the American students. Moral corruption was a forgone conclusion should such a disaster occur. She and her sister had been accepted because, and only because, of their Greek heritage. Her decision to divorce would be blamed on her lax, inferior, American value system. Mexican women rarely divorced. In her parent's eyes, Greek women weren't supposed to divorce either. She was condemned.

She remembered being at a wedding in Nogales several years before with some company from Culiacan. They had been three couples walking together through the lobby of the ranch house where the wedding was being held when one of her friends espied her twenty-some-year-old son talking to a young blonde woman who looked overtly American. She called him over and spoke to him sharply. *"No te acercas a este muchacha. Es Americana. Ya sabes que tienen custumbres muy differentes a nosotros. No te conviene. Hay muchas muchachas conocidas aqui. No tienes necesidad de estar hablando con ese tipo de muchacha." "Si mama. Te entendi. No te preocupas,"* he responded. She was warning him off possible corruption. She didn't even want him to talk to the girl, and he wasn't about to go against his mother's wishes. In their world, somebody they "knew" was always superior, it didn't matter what their family was like, as long as they knew something about them already. Unknown quantities were "bad," known quantities were "good." It seemed that he had learned his family's lesson well, because within the next year the boy had married a young woman from a locally prominent and very wealthy Mexican family. She was already five months pregnant with his first child.

♦ ♦ ♦

She had been one of a pair even before she married. They had been two girls. Two sisters. Her parents, her traditional Greek parents, had produced two daughters. When Angela was born, her uncle had said to her father, "That's too bad. Too bad for you that you had a girl. Maybe the next one will be a boy." He was the second brother, next in line to her father, and reveled in rubbing in the fact that his big brother hadn't been man enough to father a son. Her father hadn't needed a son. Angela was his first-born, and she was his progeny, named after his mother and so like his family in appearance and in character that it was understood that she was his continuity and the son he never had. A second child, another girl, was born three years later, her features and character more like her mother's family, and, despite all their protestations to the contrary, new battle lines in their small family were drawn.

> We were two sisters of one race.

Her mother and father elevated the competition between themselves to a destructive level that would forever warp them as a couple, and their daughters as sisters, into powerful, subliminally segregated camps. She hadn't understood for years that this had to do with gender, continuity and domination.

It wasn't just that she was younger; she was the quieter child, the "good" girl, with an easier, less demanding character. Her mother constantly told her as a little girl what a comfort she was, what a consolation for *everything*. Even as a small child, her female role as caretaker was established, only to continue as she grew into a woman. As the years passed and the resentment grew, she could often feel herself screaming inside, "But there's no one to look after me!" She always knew that her mother saw her as her continuity, the progeny that would carry on her side of the family genetics. It became especially important to get everything right— everything— so that her mother could be proud. How she looked, how she lived, what she was, how she cooked, how she raised her children, her marriage, her nails, her haircut, her skin, how she dressed, where she went; everything had to be better, much better than what her mother had or was. It was out of love of course— but it was an exhausting legacy to live up to. Exhausting. The weight of her mother's pride.

The summer of 2000, when she had confronted Nacho with his behaviour and found her father less than supportive, she had been shocked. She had assumed that her father would want to protect her and that he would unconditionally take her side when she asked for his support. But he hadn't; he had believed Nacho's account of the situation. Nacho had yet to understand that he had done anything out of line. In his world how he behaved was the norm and she was the one who was wrong. A year had passed. Counseling, classes, courses, self-help books, therapy, school. She had known, but Nacho hadn't, that he had a year. She had a date in her mind and it was July of 2001. She needed to see what he was willing to do to keep her. May of 2001 brought an insurmountable impasse. They decided to separate. Angela knew. Angela had known the whole time, that whole year, what was going on. From the counseling to the tears, from the anger to the frustration, Angela had heard from her step by step what she was going through. She was her sister and she listened. She never empathized though. She never said, "I know what you're going through. Chilo is the same." She never said, "I know what you're feeling, I feel like that at times." She never said, "I understand your situation. Ours is similar." Nothing. Nothing. Not until the day in May when she and Nacho decided to separate. That same day, when she phoned her mother-in-law to tell her that she needed her help, that Nacho was being unreasonable, that she and Nacho were going to separate because he was abusive, jealous, insecure and paranoid, and her mother-in-law said, *"Por que ustedes son asi? Les dieron todo. Ustedes..."* and she had interrupted. *"Ustedes quien?"* *"Ustedes. Tu y Angela."* She hadn't understood what Angela had to do with the problem *"Yo no estoy hablando por Angela. Estoy hablando por mi matrimonio, por Nacho y mi. Porque inclues al Angela?"* *"Por que Anglea dejo a Chilo hoy. Que tienen ustedes?"* It was like a bomb had dropped. She had been dumbfounded. What had happened here? How could have Angela have left Chilo at the very same time? The very same day? It wasn't possible. She had never mentioned that she was unhappy over the past year. Her mother-in-law continued, saying they had been nobodies. They had come to Mexico and married into the best family. They had been given a "name." They had been nobodies and now they were members of "high society" in Culiacan thanks to her sons, thanks to their wealth, thanks to the privilege that had been laid on their heads, now that they had "money." Where would they would have been if not for her family? They would have married some bums off the streets of Vancouver if it hadn't been for her sons. She and Angela had everything. It was impossible to make her understand. She broke in, "Things don't make people happy. You had money. You have money. You have a lot of money. You are one of the most unhappy women I know and have been since the day I met you. If money makes people so happy, why aren't you?" She had interrupted the matriarch of the family twice. She had talked back to her. She had upset her. And Aspacia had been listening on the other line. She now had an army of people against her. In Mexico, in Culiacan, in their family, this was a death wish. You did not cross them; you did not talk back to elders. You did not speak the truth. She had stepped out of her role as a woman who knew her place, and she would never be forgiven for that. Ever. Even her own family would use that incident against her. Angela, her mother, her father, would remind her of her disgraceful behaviour for the next two years as proof of how unbalanced, how horrible a person she was. She deserved everything that was coming to her because she had broken "the rules."

My sense of incompleteness, of being outside the constraints of society.

She decided to keep trying. The two families were so closely linked. If her own fell apart at the same time as Angela's, it was going to be a disaster for everyone, for the parents, for the cousins. Someone had to keep it together. She was the stronger of the two. She would be fine. She could do it. She would make it work.

It had been Nicholas's graduation. They had been visiting Vancouver, and she went to Vancouver Island to pick him up from school. He was too smart not to know that something was wrong. She had thought that she was doing the right thing by keeping their family together; she had thought that she was doing the right thing. Stephanie was thirteen, Nicholas just turned eighteen. She had wanted to give them the perfect family so badly. She had created three different homes for them, one in Nogales, one in Culiacan and the last, better than the other two, the last one a "masterpiece" to help them feel safe, to create the illusion of a wonderful life. And it had worked to a degree for all of them, even though it had almost destroyed her. She and Nicholas talked and talked on the ferry ride back to the mainland. She apologized to him, crying, saying that she was so sorry, that she had wanted it to work out, that she had tried and tried but she couldn't do it. They stood on the car deck waiting for the ferry to dock, and, as their car was first in line, they stood behind the chain barrier, looking at the rushing water glistening in the sunlight, at the approaching shoreline, as she told her son that she needed to leave his father in order to survive.

Two years later she would look back to that afternoon with him as affirmation that she had done the right thing. She was teaching her children through her choices, though only the future would show whether she had made the right one. The moment she was sure she was teaching them to choose the best path was when Nicholas said to her, "I know how Dad treats you, Mom. I know. Dad needs to learn that he has to treat my mother the way he wants me to treat my wife." If Nicholas was so sure of that, he would have to eventually understand that everything she and his father did set a precedent, and that he, Thano, Stephanie, her parents and Nacho's family had to understand that to treat her the way Nacho did was not acceptable. The way her father treated her mother was not acceptable. The way Nacho's father had treated Nacho's mother was not acceptable, the way her father had sometimes treated her, his daughter, was not acceptable. This was the end of the line. She was the end of the line. Her children would know that men and women were not equal in many of their abilities, but they did have equal rights. She hoped that she, her daughter and her sons were going to be able do things differently, to be able to teach themselves, learn from others, and be able to create a new value system, a value system without precedent in their families.

> Time makes more converts than reason.

♦♦♦

She settled herself deep into the soft, down cushions of the sofa and picked up the embroidered pillow to look at it more closely. All her mother's work had been transformed into a tangible artifact that would outlast her and be handed down for generations. It was as tradition should be, a piece of family history, a legacy of a family and a home that her mother had been part of, that she had contributed to, and that she, as her daughter was tied to.

The pillow she held was the female pug, and her Elizabethan dress had an elaborate ruffle of fine lace that framed her head. She had bought the pillow patterns in a charming little shop in the old quarter of New Orleans several years ago. The shop's owner had chatted with her as she wrapped up her purchase, commenting that many of her customers were now men, as they had found the art of embroidery to be a therapeutic and relaxing hobby.

Chapter FIFTEEN

THE MIRROR

She sat in the tufted chair next to the fire with her book unopened on her lap, staring out the glass-paned doors, their reflection darkened by the setting sun, at the honeysuckle-draped columns beyond. She didn't have the energy to get up and go outside; it felt like the house withheld her, inside, close to it. It held her in because without her it would no longer be the same. It needed her life source to come alive. Without her it would be empty of its soul. She had been the creator, had created its persona, and now it was reluctant to relinquish her, as was Nacho, both of them draining her life force to feed themselves. She had given to both freely, without thought of the bargain she was striking, until she began to resent that which they took without return. She gave to her children as well, but that energy renewed and revived her, regenerated her, because it was whole in and of itself, given of her, not taken.

Nacho and the children thought that the house would be the same without her; that the house was an entity in and of itself. But she knew better and the house knew better. It would never be the same.

Last summer, July of 2002, they had received a phone call at five o'clock in the morning. Nacho's niece, Lulu, his eldest sister's third daughter, had been killed in a car accident in the early morning, when her fiancée of a few hours, drunk after hours of celebrating their new engagement, crashed into a lightpost on the river walk in Culiacan. They had both been killed instantly; Lulu, a young widow of thirty, was flung out of the car, leaving her six-year-old girl an orphan in the care of her grandmother, Nacho's sister, who was battling a rare cancer.

They had flown down to the double funeral, shaken that the life of this young woman had been taken so tragically just as she had grasped at a chance to rebuild it. She had been a sweet and generous young girl who had become pregnant at twenty, an awful social stigma in any young girl's life, becoming an unwed mother, "*ante la socieded.*" She had become a widow two years later when her husband was killed. Her social standing should have buried her alive, but she had found a young man to love her, marry her and adopt her child. Now the little girl had no parents, the happy news that she would have a new father shattered like her mother's body.

After spending hours in the same funeral parlour that had held the body of Lulu's grandfather, they had all gone to Nacho's sister's house. The large family that now had great-grandchildren, one an orphan, sat throughout the large living room as everyone tried to be as normal a possible for the children's sake. Those who needed to cry left the room.

I shall pass through this world but once. If, therefore, there be any kindness I can show, or any good thing I can do, let me do it now; let me not defer it or neglect it, for I shall not pass this way again.

She had been sitting, conversing with Nacho's nieces, facing an ornate, gold-framed mirror, when she saw Nacho walk up behind her, both of them captured in its refection. She saw that he held something above her head. "What is that?" she asked. "It's a pendulum." "What's a pendulum?" "I'm not sure, but it's supposed to move when you hold it over someone. That's what they told me. I guess it doesn't work," he added as the pendulum hung down, perfectly still, over her head. She saw him move about the room, holding it over different members of the family. Sometimes it moved gently, sometimes not, making it unclear if its movement was natural, or caused by some unintentional motion. Someone took it from Nacho to try themselves, and excited exclamations were heard as it moved in a circular motion. Everyone wanted to try it and eventually it came to her. She had no belief in the paranormal and held it disinterestedly over one of the nieces. It moved strongly in a repeated circle. She was surprised. She stilled it with her hand and tried again. It began to move again. She was intrigued. She held it over Nicholas, Stephanie, Thano, nieces, nephews, sister-in-laws. Anyone and everyone she held it over, it moved, some moreso than others. With the other family members, for some it had moved and not for others; for her it moved consistently, sometimes more strongly and quickly, in a broader circle, with a faster motion, sometimes less so, but there was a connection she had, an energy that was physically visible that was manifesting itself with this small metal drop. She held it over Nacho; it moved in a circle over him, too.

You go not, till I set you up a glass Where you may see the innermost part of you.

"What's it doing?" "It's moving," she replied. "You're moving it. Stand in front of the mirror. The mirror doesn't lie. I bet you're moving your hand." "Fine. You're right. The mirror doesn't lie." Nacho sat in a chair in front of the mirror and she held the pendulum over his head. She steadied her arm against her side. The pendulum began to move in slow, steady circles above his head. Their eyes met in the mirror and they both knew it was a moment of truth. There was no balance between them; what she gave was not what she received. Not even close. The mirror didn't lie.

Any idea or thought that is held in the mind, has a tendency to direct the physical body to transform such thoughts or ideas into their material equivalents.

She thought of that moment just ten months ago as she looked to the right of the door. There hung a perfectly square mirror, not very large, with a frame that sloped down and away from the raised pane of smoky glass. She had chosen it because the eerie effect the shaded mirror created had appealed to her, reflecting the room it was in, yet transforming it at the same time into something else, the place she sat darkened, changed, other. Behind her hung another mirror, almost of the same proportion, but rectangular. They hung directly across from one another. Depending upon where she stood, they reflected one another or not. Where she stood determined if she could even see herself or if she was lost beyond the frame of the glass to another dimension... without her. It was a world of things without human warmth, a world where she didn't exist except as a shadow.

> Eyes I dare not meet in dreams.

There was a tall cabinet with carved capitals and pale wood columns at the end of the room, standing almost floor to ceiling, the cabinet doors that hid the equipment behind them paneled with plates of long, rectangular, beveled mirrors. They too, reflected the room in a way that transformed as well as reflected, including her or hiding her presence, according to her need to be seen or felt.

> What the artist can match... is only "appearances;" his is the world of mirrors that deceive the eye.

She had mirrors on cabinet fronts, mirror panels instead of wood on furniture, and an oval mirror with a silver-gilt frame hanging above the fireplace in the living room. Each one had its own character and its method of metamorphosis. The antique mirror, mercury-stained with age, took the room it reflected and merged it back in time as a sepia stain did to a photograph. The powder room had a massive, gold frame crowned with a cherub that dominated the small space where it hung, its mirrored surface reflecting the imposing space of the atrium outside the small room, marrying the two rooms in one frame. A long mirror with a hand-painted garland of flowers reflected the pink rosebud chintz of Stephanie's room, its beveled mirror edge creating a transposition, not a copy, of the room reflected there. Nicholas had two mirrors that reflected the pair of beds in his room, the golden, gilded, wood sunbursts holding twin-curved, convex, circles of mirror that reflected the room's contents in a distorted version of another reality. Thano's room had no mirrors. He had an uncanny ability to see what was real. The mirrors just made it more difficult for him to avoid what hurt. He couldn't use them to escape as she did.

> Desiring truth, awaiting it, laboriously distilling a few words, forever desiring... truth.

It was the massive metal-frame doors that separated the atrium from the bedrooms, the public area of the house from the private, that trapped her every time she passed through their portal, capturing her in a surface that was symbol, reality and illusion, truth and fiction, as she knew that to go beyond the surface was a test, a test of movement. Whenever she didn't want to see, she shifted her head slightly, moved through the doors without looking and ignored the disclosures of her world that the doors held as they swung open and shut, their creaking weight, mercurial finish and handsome, bronze, frames disguising her life and her family's life from the world outside. The doors reflected what the world wanted to see: a beautiful home, a beautiful family and a world of privilege. The doors reflected a perfect world that saw only glimpses of reality, sadness, pain and anger. Those that saw the truth had to be quick, before it was disguised again in a flash of glass.

> Echo or mirror
> seeking of itself
> And makes a toy of
> thought.

The doors held images that brought glimpses of joy and love as well. They held in their surfaces reflections of Thano, Nicholas and herself, sitting on the sofa in the hallway, talking and laughing for hours as Stephanie and Nacho slept in their rooms. So many conversations had passed in that hallway into the early morning hours, the three of them talking about friends, about problems, about girls, about dreams, about heartache, about school, about life. Those long nights were some of the happiest she had known, and those memories were going to be amongst the most difficult to leave in the door's care, as were the images of Stephanie in pigtails rollerblading around the big room and Nicholas playing basketball against its walls before the heart of the house, the atrium, had furniture and art to disguise the emptiness with things.

Mirrors, mirrors... everywhere. She had chosen them, placed them, to enhance a room, enhance a piece of furniture, enhance, transform her life. In the mirror, the world she saw wasn't the world she lived in. It was beyond her reality. It was prettier there, empty of sadness, empty of pain, empty of her life, playing a game of psychological chaos, a world of conscious make-believe where illusion held its own image. Her retina held one image, but her mind created something else, something better. Unless she chose to stand in front of the mirror; then there was no escape. Then what the mirror reflected was what she lived. If she stood in front of the mirror. She couldn't make use of the illusion and watch it at the same time. It would betray her, if she weren't careful. If she stood in front of the mirror. So she chose not to.

> **Artists create the world they imagine.**

The mirror was supposed to reflect the self, the ostensible outer self, the body. The more illusive inner being, the self that was seen in the glimpse of an expression, the look in an eye, the attention to image, or not, was what the mirror invited, tempted and reflected. The acceptance of self, image or not, was what only the mirror knew. At one point she had said to Nacho, "Only you can look in the mirror and know what you see there. You are the only one that doesn't see the illusion, that knows the truth, that knows the secrets, and the truth is, you don't like what you see, you don't like who you are. That's why you treat me the way that you do."

That was why the mirror both fascinated and repelled. She had never enjoyed looking in the mirror at herself.

> **Why despite all our mirrors, do we never really know what we look like?**

Even on a good day, the mirror wasn't her friend, but a harsh judge and jury that found her wanting. She had learned long ago, before she even had conscious memory, that good girls couldn't make mistakes, that pretty girls were always supposed to be pretty; that someone else was always better, smarter, prettier, and that she had to work very hard to be smart enough, good enough, pretty enough to meet the high standards her family held. It was Angela, her sister, who made mistakes and whose mistakes were part and parcel of who she was. Because she was the first, it was accepted, if aggravating, that that was just the way she was. She, on the other hand, the second child, the last child, tried to do and be everything right so that her parents wouldn't worry, so that they wouldn't be upset. That was why she had to be perfect. The perfect family, the perfect home, perfect health, the perfect life were what she showed the world and what the world believed. She knew what that image cost her. One day, as she and her father discussed Angela and her problems, both personal and physical, he said, "You don't have to deal with the same issues. Look at you, you're perfect." She had been so hurt. He may as well have told her that she was a monster. What she heard was that her father didn't want her to have any problems, that she was inhuman, without needs, without need of his support or help. She was fine, she was always fine. Angela always needed his help and support, his loyalty. He always felt protective toward Angela but always expected her to be fine. She had to be.

> **POST HOC ERGO PROPTER HOC**
>
> **Before this, because of this.**

That summer evening in 2000 when she walked in the door of her parent's home in Vancouver after her confrontation with Nacho, her father had been disbelieving when she told him she wanted his help. She had told him that she and Nacho had problems, huge problems, and had had for years. "But you looked all right," her father protested. "You never said anything. Why now? You looked like you were happy. I mean, your mother said things to me sometimes, but all couples have problems. It can't be true. Nacho says that you are the problem. Why are you being difficult?" The wound she had felt when he had believed Nacho had been twofold: the one wound, because of his lack of loyalty, the second, caused by her own shame that she had finally told her father what her life was really like, only to be disbelieved. She had asked for his help, only to be dismissed. At that point she had not felt a mother or a wife, but a daughter looking to her father for his protection. It had been a harsh reflection of what life in a patriarchal family meant, even in the twenty-first century. Nacho's word had been accepted and *trusted*, not hers, because in this world "men knew what they were dealing with and woman exaggerated and were emotional."

> **Creations of the mind, not pictures of the real world.**

The mirror was used as a metaphor of truth in the study of symbolism. Whatever was reflected therein was an unadulterated version of what stood before it. She had chosen to play a game with truth, a game with image. She had a wall in the hallway that was covered in frames, pretty frames made of wood with gilt, frames that were round, square, oval, rectangular... all empty. This collection of frames had no pictures in them and no mirrors either. They were just frames. They had no stories to tell, no images to reflect, no illusions to escape into. They just were. She knew that that was where she needed to go. Not to be empty but just to be. Not as a reflection, not as anyone's image of her, but as she was. Unadorned.

She thought back to those first years in Nacho's family, back to before she had even met him, to the time she met Aspacia. She had admired Aspacia's beauty and charisma with the hero worship only a thirteen year old was capable of, and it hadn't been until years and years later that she eventually realized her to be spoiled and narcissistic. Growing up in Canada in an Anglo culture, she had learned by osmosis that looking too long in a mirror was a sign of vanity. Her Greek family had taught her that feeling attractive was conceit, that taking care of oneself instead of always putting others first was selfish. It had seemed that Aspacia had no such inhibitions. Mirrors were meant to assure herself of her attractive appearance at every opportunity, and she took it as a given that she came first and foremost. Her appearance, not her substance, was what was most important to her. It was what garnered her the attention she craved. Creams, perfumes, lotions, dress, all played an important role in her and every member of her family's lives. They were famous in Culiacan for their attractive appearance. The stories of their mother's infamous beauty as a young woman, and of how that beauty had captured the eye of the Greek immigrant twenty years her senior, were legendary. Their mother's beauty had achieved an importance worthy of founding a family, a family that esteemed appearance highly. Body parts: eyes, hair, figure, dress. These were all favorite topics of conversation whenever the family was together. Anyone who crossed their paths was subject to their dissection.

Those that live in front of the mirror and those that live behind it.

Whenever they were in Mexico, she, Nacho, Thano, Nicholas and Stephanie constantly heard what the others opinioned about their physiques, their eyes, their hair, their "beauty." In a country where the indigenous peoples were short, dark and physically unprepossessing, much was made of light skin, light eyes, light hair and European background. These were intangible assets that could not be purchased and were highly valued, convening a social status without price.

Mirror, mirror on the wall.

It had taken her years to understand that her appearance was her most valuable attribute to Nacho, her figure as much as her face. He hadn't had a picture of her on his desk or in his wallet for years, only of the children, until finally she had framed one for him. It had been a picture of nothing more than her face looking at the camera. He had gotten the message, and later, after some nineteen years of marriage, had put a photo of her under the glass on his bureau too, a picture of her at the beach in her bathing suit. It had seemed significant to her that that was the picture of her that he chose above any other.

Shadows of things, into things... into truth.

As she sat back in her chair and looked about her, the mirrors on the wall and on the cabinet became the curious keys to her mind. In the world she had created, she had tried to escape the life she felt trapped in, the flashes of silver glass offering her portals through which she could remove herself from her reality. In those other worlds, everything was possible and nothing intolerable as she found other avenues to slowly arrive at the truth of who she was and what she needed. Now she had understood enough about who she was to determine to live her life, not escape from it.

Whatever games are played with us, we must play no games with ourselves, but deal in our privacy with the last honesty and truth.

Chapter SIXTEEN

THE MONEY

The Christmas tree was up again. She walked past the pinpoints of lights that faded on and off, past the bright wooden ornaments that she had stopped collecting long ago, the garlands of bright red cranberries, the elegant bands of red, green and gold ribbon: all the same ornaments that appeared at Christmastime, every year. What was different was that underneath, the tree was empty.

Christmas Eve was just six nights away. Presents weren't wrapped yet, weren't under the tree yet, weren't tantalizing those who walked by with their presence or promise of what they held under the tissue and paper yet. She had three bags of gifts for the children that she had collected from Lay Away in her closet, paid for with a gnawing anxiety that Nacho wouldn't reimburse her for the money she had spent, just as he had been remiss about paying her back for so many of her expenses for the last six months. When they began to battle over the dissolution of their marriage, Nacho had left for Los Angles to better avoid the inevitable. He had been there since September: his justification was that he was working on a new business.

No one does wrong willingly.

Anyone who knew she was getting divorced was more than happy to share their own stories of woe with her; one friend in Tucson was living in a one bedroom with three hundred dollars a month rent. She had no car and took the bus to work. She had also tried to commit suicide two months ago, as her eldest son raged at her for abandoning them and destroying their family's stability, even though her one bedroom was six houses away from them, and all of her income except for bus fare and basic necessities went to their upkeep. Her soon to be ex chose not to work.

There was her sister, Angela, in Vancouver living on a paltry allowance, financially punished for leaving her husband. She now worked at Starbucks because she had no work experience or academic degree to support her in getting a better paying job. Angela said that Chilo paid the housekeeper in Culiacan more than she earned every month. There was her other friend who had left her husband ten years ago after living a life of privilege, now sustaining herself by selling gifts and accessories from her home. She earned enough to barely get by and paid all of her own overhead and personal expenses after having lived all of her life as a dependent. Her sons and daughter were supported by their father in the lifestyle to which they were accustomed, but she had left him, so she got nothing. He had a new woman to keep him company for years, while she lived in Monterrey, eeking out a living. She had still not divorced and her husband provided no financial support for her after twenty-six years of marriage. There was another woman who had told her that she had left the house to her husband, the house that she had created for their family, so that his girlfriend could move in with an allowance four times what she got as alimony. She had been diagnosed as being bi-polar shortly after their divorce, and had a very difficult time adjusting to not having her daughters around and being financially self-sufficient. She had feared for her ability to support herself, but she was on her own and surviving, while her ex-husband lived in her old home with his new girlfriend and their daughters, a prominent citizen of the Southern Arizona community. There was another woman who broke into tears every time she told her story, even though she insisted that she was far happier than she had been.

And how do you make your living?

You make your living by being married.

She told of how her wealthy husband had decimated her financially when she divorced him, taking her car, her jewelry and home, changing the locks on their Tucson home. She now had a job working for the minimum wage as she tried to rebuild her life at forty-eight years of age. All this, after having lived a life of financial privilege and emotional destitution. There was another friend who had decided to divorce her alcoholic husband after twenty-five years of physical and mental abuse. She had raised their four daughters, only to be given one-thirtieth of what he was worth to get her to move on and leave him alone, in her house, with her furniture and possessions and his new girlfriend. She took care of her daughters in Tucson on her own, as she always had, while he partied and bar hopped with his family's money as though he were a reborn twenty-year old. There was another woman who had lived with her son in a Tucson shelter to get away from her husband for three months, in order to escape from a husband who regularly beat her, her friend who had been taken to Morocco by her husband, been drugged and beaten with a baseball bat; who had escaped with the clothes on her back in order to get away. There must be women who had come out of divorce emotionally intact with or without a fair financial settlement, but she didn't know any personally, or even anecdotally.

Perhaps the greatest social service that can be rendered by anybody to the country and to mankind is to bring up a family; but here again, because there is nothing to sell, there is a general disposition to regard a married woman's work as no work at all, and to take it as a matter of course that she should not be paid for it.

As she sat on the stone steps and watched the lights brighten and dim, she thought of the day the marriage counselor had told her and Nacho, as they sat in his office, that there were four basic ingredients that kept a relationship together, four basic needs that had to be met for both parties to be, at the least satisfied, and at best, content and happy. "You need your emotional, intellectual, material and sexual needs to be met or the relationship will start to falter. When one goes, it will start to limp, but it will still function. When two go, there's trouble. When three go, you're in crisis, and when the fourth goes, it's dead." Her emotional needs had been unmet from the beginning. Before they were even married, she had denied herself the emotional sustenance that she had craved from Nacho. She had denied it, belittled it and even destroyed it to stay in the marriage, sabotaging herself. Her emotional needs had been filled through her children. Her intellectual needs had been kept alive, barely, by her voracious reading, until she went back to university. Then she had been consumed with feeding herself with ideas, thoughts and enjoying intellectual companionship. Nacho hadn't been her intellectual companion, he had been her intellectual enemy, denying and belittling her intellect because he feared that part of her. She had been tragically misled from the very beginning, led to believe that those crucial parts of her would be cherished and nurtured by him, choosing a relationship that wouldn't nourish her.

When her father had left her at the altar on her wedding day, he had said to Nacho, "Take care of her." Nacho had remembered the moment well over the years; it had really made an impact on him, perhaps because he knew that he couldn't live up to his promise from the beginning, except for the day-to-day financial matters.

Happiness does not depend on wealth.

He would declare adamantly that he had taken care of her, using the fact he had provided for her financially as validation of his honour. Her father's comment had made an impact on her as well; to her it had meant that Nacho was to empower, support, give her tenderness and understanding, not just money and the accoutrements it provided.

They had spent New Years together a second time the year she was sixteen. Her family had gone to Culiacan again after their beach vacation farther south. That evening had begun in another grand ballroom, in a crowd elegantly dressed in tuxedos and long dresses, the women laden with status jewelry, the men cologned, combed and starched as they walked about under the crystal chandeliers. She and Nacho had been absorbed in each other, oblivious to the drunken comments and loud conversations around their table. She had been sixteen to his twenty-two that year, as they had forayed into that eternal game of intellectual foreplay that attracted females and males into a courting ritual, a game of disclosure and revelation that exposed interests, culture, character and beliefs. She had been sitting next to him, when she asked," "What do you like in a girl?" "I like dark hair, someone pretty and someone who's intelligent," he had replied. "Intelligent," was the word she had hung onto. She had discounted the rest of his criteria as being unimportant, because they were unimportant to her, but they weren't unimportant to him. She just hadn't paid enough attention to his value system. She had wanted him to admire her for what she valued in herself; she didn't want to be admired for her appearance. The words had been enticing, though his actions would later prove him to hate the very things he professed to admire. They learned together that he loved and hated her appearance, that he loved and hated her intellect, that he loved and hated her talent, her honesty— in fact, everything about her, everything, he loved, he hated, and that was what tortured both of them every day. It depended on the day, on the moment, whether love or hate was in play.

One of the strongest motives that leads man to art... is escape from everyday life with its painful crudity and hopeless dreariness from the fetters of... everyday... A finely tempered nature longs to escape from personal life into the world of objective thought and perception.

The second ingredient, the intellectual, that was necessary for their survival as a partnership, was always missing, but she didn't know it. For so many years she had chatted away in the car when they drove back and forth to Tucson, telling him about a novel, an article or another type of book she had read. She soon noticed that it was always her talking, sharing, teaching, while he listened. Eventually it came to the point where he would disparage what she had said, even if he knew nothing about it, just to prove to her that he could. She had hated that, the fact that she couldn't talk to him.

Do their best to change you
They can't erase you

It seemed that Nacho's perception of female sexuality was catastrophically confused as well. In his world a sexual woman was a bad woman. Good women didn't really enjoy or want sex; they had sex to please their husbands and to have children. She had heard, from the females in his family, and from many others in Mexico over the years, that women who enjoyed or wanted sex, who were comfortable with their bodies, were depraved, licentious or just bad. It was "common knowledge" that almost all the men had affairs outside of their marriage and that the women they went after were prostitutes, bank tellers or office help, women who were not part of their society. These women were culturally accepted as being sexual in a way that a wife could not be. Many of the wives she knew spoke of "headaches," going to bed in the dark so their husband wouldn't "see" them, of not having sex while pregnant, turning him away because he was "over sexed," not having sex because they didn't want to get pregnant, and, being Catholic, not wanting to take birth control. A wife who was sexual was man hungry, a viper, a black widow, the type of woman who was insatiable and on the prowl for a victim to satisfy her. This perception of female sexuality wasn't just limited to Latin American culture; she had seen it in the "noir films" she had studied at school as well. She saw it also in the comments from the young men around her. They were disgusted by girls that had multiple sexual partners, even as they applauded themselves for being manly and doing the same thing.

> **Whoever sets out to persuade men to accept a new idea, but as a truth that is felt, should know beforehand that the human mind is not a blank sheet, on which one can write with ease, and should not therefore grieve or despair when he finds that people do not pay attention to him.**

That she had wanted to be with Nacho from the beginning had not been a good thing in his eyes. If she wanted him, well then, who else might she not want? His insecurity made him believe that it was only a matter of time before he would bore her, then she would be looking for someone else. Of course, that was his projection again, but it caused so many tears and recriminations between them, so much destruction, so much pain. She later found out that he had been unfaithful almost from the beginning of their marriage, friends were finally free to tell her of his encounters with women who were easy, familiar and undemanding. In-and-out encounters that meant nothing except betrayal and lack of self. A relationship required work, a few hours, a few minutes, or a one-night-stand didn't. The relationship was missing the third ingredient, even though she couldn't see it. She had convinced herself that the intimacy and love that Nacho couldn't show in any other way but in their bed was enough. She now saw that the third element needed to sustain their relationship was critically damaged from the beginning. According to the professional analysis of what a marriage was, their relationship never had a chance.

Then came the forth and final ingredient, the financial. Money. A relationship reduced to a monetary value didn't work, at least not for her, even though she had seen many over the years ready to strike that bargain. A relationship where money was a secret weapon didn't work. A relationship where money was used to wield power didn't work. A relationship where money was given and taken like a yo-yo, to control, didn't work. A relationship where a person or persons based their self esteem on their financial assets was doomed to be locked into a corrupt, degrading value system that would erode everything around it like a cancer. With divorce, that was all that was left of a relationship that had once meant emotional, physical and intellectual commitment. It was reduced to numbers. How much was each of them going to get in order to live separate lives? For the majority of men, they considered the money to be theirs. They had gone to work each day to earn it, the wife had not.

To most people, the word success and the word money are synonymous.

She had later heard from Nicholas that his father couldn't spend time with Stephanie when she was home on break because he was working. She took it as an implied criticism that his father worked, and she did not.

"Does a person who sits at a desk all day, using a computer, work, Nicholas?" she had joked. "Or would you only consider it work if he was the president of Microsoft? How about the women that clean the house? They get paid for it, so that's considered work, but if I do the same thing, it's not, because I am not financially reimbursed for it. That's just part of my non-paid, or slave labour, as a mother. Likewise, if they clean a closet, clean the floor, water plants, it is considered to be work, for the very simple reason that their work is recognized by giving it a monetary value. If I am not paid for my work, it is not valued, whether I am a mother, a wife, an artist or a garbage collector. Mind you, I did not really realize the consequences of giving my labour freely, but I got shafted because *I* didn't value my work enough to give a value to it. I don't think that anybody, after putting in twenty-two years with a company, be it family owned or not, would say, "Well, I enjoyed that. It was great while it lasted. You keep the increase in value to the company we have built together as your own, just because I know you don't want to share. I have some clothes that I'll take, my dignity and satisfaction for a job well done, and the rest is yours, because you never told me that the contract I signed when I took this job took away my rights to anything I would create together with you. I don't want to be bitter, so, you just keep it. Somehow, I have a very hard time imagining your father doing that. Ever." She thought of the night she had asked him for the divorce, of what a sweet, romantic scene it had been, and then about what she was dealing with now.

In April, when Nacho had told her that he was going to cut off her credit cards, she had been furious that he could still try to control her in any way, even though they had been living apart for four months, even though she no longer wanted to be his wife and wanted her severance pay, her retirement, social security, whatever it was to be called, so that she could separate herself from him and move on with her life. She deeply resented that he would still try to control her, even when she wasn't in his presence. She could still be upset by him devaluing her efforts as mother, wife, housekeeper, chef, social secretary, jeweler, travel agent, tutor, interior decorator, furniture manufacturer, personal valet, caterer, gardener, student, designer, therapist. The thoughts, the words that she had shared with him months ago, "I will always love you," were impossible to keep present in the face of what she saw as a personal attack, an attack meant to cripple her financially, to keep her weak and dependent.

> **How can a man be at once free and forced to conform to wills which are not his own?**

That weekend in April, she went out from morning till night all day Friday, Saturday and Sunday morning, knowing that they were going to meet for lunch "to discuss matters" Sunday afternoon. She began at Home Depot, went to furniture stores, art galleries, a lighting store, a clothing boutique, the cosmetic department at Dillard's, Best Buy for electronics. She bought anything she could think of that she wanted or might want or need in the next year. She went to the townhouse in Tucson and unloaded bags and bags of things and put all the delivery orders for the bigger items into a folder. As she walked through the door of the restaurant Sunday afternoon and saw Nacho sitting at a table in the window, she was still thinking of where to install the flat screen television that Best Buy would be delivering next week, along with her stereo and satellite dish system. She sat down and smiled at Nacho. "How are you?" "Fine, and you?" "Fine." "How have you been?" "Oh, busy, you know me. I'm finishing my thesis, studying for exams, writing final papers and then I had some errands to do this weekend." "Yeah, me too. I've been busy at the office finishing up the season. You know that you can't use your cards after today?" "Yes, but I was wondering, will you be using yours?" "Well, I have to. I have responsibilities for the kids, for the house. Of course I need to use mine. You don't need anything." She thought of his Porsche sitting in the garage at the house that he drove once a month at best, of their closet the size of most bedrooms, of the racks of undrunk wine in the basement, the plane tickets used every month as the family moved from Tucson to Culiacan to Los Angeles to Vancouver, the gardener, the housekeepers, the supplies needed for the upkeep of the house, the boys' apartment in Phoenix, their fleet of family cars, and nodded her head in agreement. "Of course, I understand. You need money and I don't." Their lunch ended in a quiet argument that those at other tables couldn't overhear, about the divorce, about money, about the children, about ending their life together. When she left the restaurant, she was simmering with frustration, and by the time she got home, she was crying. And crying and crying. She had wanted to hear an acknowledgment, some appreciation for the three fine children she had brought up, for her impeccable home, for the delicious meals, for the academic success she had achieved, for her commitment, loyalty and love, for the professional success she had earned. She still wanted a validation from him that everything she had done, she had done passionately and well. The tears were because she would never hear those words, and no matter how much she spent, it would never make Nacho value her. She loaded the bags back into the car and spent the next two days taking everything back. The young man at Best Buy almost broke into tears at losing his sale of the year, but she felt so much better. Nacho hadn't won. She hadn't lost herself in his value system.

As she looked at the tree, she thought how that event had proved such a turning point. It had brought with it a deeper realization of where she had been and what she needed to shed to move forward. She stood up and turned to walk through the atrium to the family room, sat in "her" chair and turned to her left. Hanging under the small mirror was an old copper engraving titled "The Misers." The picture was of two men, dressed in medieval clothing, hunched over a table where an empty velvet sack lay among a pile of gold coins. The expression on their faces said it all. Their faces were pinched with greed, disfigured by avarice, consumed with their insatiable need for gold. The picture was a metaphorical truth, that whosoever would pursue the possession of riches for the sake of riches alone would be destroyed, that whosoever would seek riches through trickery, bribery or theft, dishonesty of any kind, would be consumed, and whosoever would be unwilling to help or reward his fellow man in his journey towards financial success would be punished, for the greed would erode all the good in his life like a cancer.

She had been very wary of the destruction she could see looming should her children grow up knowing nothing but privilege. She was acutely aware of the rarefied world they lived in, whereas they would not be, having known nothing else. If she isolated them in that world as the majority of the wealthy did, keeping their children amongst their "own kind," she would be doing them a serious disservice. In Mexico it had been impossible to counterbalance the social schism that existed between the wealthy and the poor, there was no middle ground where the chasm could be breached. The well-to-do lived in one reality and the poor, in a very different one. Because the polarity was so overwhelming, it was practically ignored. The wealthy applauded themselves for being philanthropic and employing the poor, while simultaneously teaching the next generation that they couldn't be too kind or "they" would overrun them, steal from them and get lazy, forgetting their "place." She had gone to Mississippi when she was thirteen, and her father had made sure that they went to see the shanty towns where society attempted to geographically and socially isolate the African-Americans. Growing up in Canada, she had never seen anything like it. She had been horrified at the intolerance and prejudice she saw pervade their culture, at the financial abuse of one community by the other.

Money only appeals to selfishness and always irresistibly tempts its owner to abuse it.

She later saw, as those immersed in it could not, the similarities of the Southern culture to the Latin American, saw that the lack of wealth was self perpetrating, so that it was inevitable that many of the poor became lazy, irresponsible, resentful and angry, because they knew that they were never going to get out. They were trapped in a world where it was nearly impossible to succeed in the face of the huge odds that were stacked against them. The attitude of the wealthy towards the poor and the status of women in those two cultures were extremely similar; the social cancer which enabled one society to become successful off the sweat and labour of those less fortunate contaminated the privileged, bringing them to believe in their superiority and "*droigt to reigneur.*" Of course people were aware of the disparity and injustice; they were surrounded by it while being held captive to it, for once used to living in that world, it was impossible for the wealthy to get out either. Where else could they live where there was someone to wash their car, polish their shoes, do their laundry, mop the floors, make their beds, cook their meals, look after their children and chauffeur them for pennies an hour? They became so dependent upon that infrastructure as to practically become invalids. And the money kept them there. Women stayed in marriages where they were unhappy and sons worked in family businesses that they hated. They stayed where they were, afraid to leave the life of privilege, because that was all that they knew. Because of the money.

I long to see the miseries of the world since the sight of them is necessary to happiness.

When they returned to Nogales after living in Culiacan for five years, she enrolled both boys in the local public school, instead of the local parochial school, where most of the "known families" children went, the known families being the economically privileged from the other side of the border. Nogales was a curious mixture of American and Mexican culture, though it was far more Mexican than anything else. Here people had more opportunity than in Mexico, if they managed to cross the border. Children could go to better schools, see a doctor, play sports, learn music, and learn to read in both languages. In elementary school, the optimism was obvious, though by high school, social class reared its ugly head. While young, she had wanted her children to be aware that some of their classmates dreamt of going to Disneyland just once in their lives, that they might never get past high school, if they finished that, know that their fathers worked for men like Nacho, worked in a warehouse, and they had relatives who worked in the fields in Culiacan. In Mexico, it wouldn't have been possible for children of the two social stratas to intermingle, but this was the border, a rarefied world that was neither culture, but its own. Even the way they spoke was a confused and broken mixture of English and Spanish that only those who spoke both could follow. Her children often referred to their years in that school in Nogales as an important point of reference when comparing the different worlds where they had lived from north to south on the North American continent. It became a crucible for social conscience with far more impact than having lived in Mexico or Canada alone could ever have done. Growing up in Nogales, they learned, because they lived with it, the power of paperback rank and the difference that culture made to human formation.

She knew of one couple whose every argument had been about money. He had it, he controlled it, he earned it... it was his. His wife eventually got a job and returned to work when the youngest child was old enough, simply because she was so tired of the constant financial bickering. Counselors and marital courses had taught her that it was the most common issue that couples fought and divorced over. Money. When she had heard that statistic, she had been unable to relate. There had been many issues that were hammered over between Nacho and herself, but finances had never been an issue. Except that she knew nothing of what he earned, what he saved, what he spent, where he spent it, on what or on whom. She had no real idea of his worth, and even the act of making a will had taken years of arguments and cajoling, because that meant some kind of disclosure on his behalf. Disclosure of anything outside of the house made him wild. They had been married for twenty years before he agreed to write a will, and even then she had later found out that he had never sent in property titles to the lawyers, or car titles, or any documents that would have been necessary to validate the document for their children. None. But money wasn't an issue. They had plenty; she had credit cards, as did he. Money wasn't an issue. She had title to nothing in their marriage except for the house. But money wasn't an issue. She had taken title to two cars since she had married, one, so that she could import it and drive it in Mexico. Nacho had had no choice but to give her the car, because as a foreigner, she had to drive her own vehicle. Even though she had driven six different cars in over twenty-three years, the others had been Nacho's. But money wasn't an issue. She had found out after five years of marriage that the marriage certificate that she had signed in Culiacan at the age of twenty, untranslated and unexplained, had stated that all of her new husband's holdings were his and his alone, that he had no intention of sharing them with his wife and that he would address her as a wife, when in reality she was nothing better than a concubine. He had no intention, ever, of validating her contribution to their marriage in any way except with spending money, jewelry, a new prefix and surname. She still could not see the difference between her relationship to him and a mistress's. She had even heard of his friends who had mistresses in San Diego with BMW's and waterfront town homes. What was the difference, just because she carried his name? He always considered marriage to be about sole and separate property. But money wasn't an issue. Whenever he said that he was short of money, that they couldn't afford something, if she saw him slip his nephews or one of his nieces a hundred dollar bill, she pretended that it didn't bother her. She pretended that she didn't understand that he was buying their loyalty. Because money wasn't an issue.

When he had taken the money from a property sale and gifted it to his brother three years before, even though they had agreed to buy their sons a low-cost house to live in for college with those funds, to begin building some assets for their future, things changed. Money became an issue. All the times that money hadn't been an issue acquired a new status, and all of them became ammunition to fuel her ire at the way she had been denied any voice in her financial affairs from the beginning of their marriage. Money became a huge issue, and when she asked for a divorce, it grew into a monster. Money; a monetary measure of their marriage was all that was left of twenty-two-years, and Nacho didn't consider the money to be anyone's but his.

That first year of her metamorphosis, in 2000, after months of trying to change their relationship, she had finally been exhausted. She had told Stephanie that she needed a break, that Daddy wasn't to know, but that she needed to tell her where she would be so that she wouldn't worry. She was going away for a couple of days. She had gone to an abbey twenty miles away. She had felt a need to be somewhere where she wouldn't talk or interact with anyone else, and these nuns had taken a vow not to talk unless necessary. The thought of nuns comforted her, they had nothing but good associations for her from her years at the Convent, and she needed to feel safe, be somewhere that was completely unmaterialistic, so that she could focus on her thoughts and feelings. The second day she was there, she sat outside in the sun, heat beating down on her as she watched two small lizards wrestle in the dust. A small, old nun had come along and begun to hoe the bed of roses bordering the pavers. There was an electric wire that ran around the perimeter of the rose bed, and she had asked, "Sister, what is the electric fence for?" "The deer come at night and eat the roses until there is nothing left but the stems. The poor roses, they try to defend themselves by growing bigger thorns to keep the deer away. They try to protect themselves from threat." She had been so struck by the nun's comment. How was it possible that even a rose had the instinct to try and to defend itself, and it was so hard for her to do the same?

She had gone back home the third day and sent Stephanie to a friend's house so that she and Nacho could talk. They went into the study. "Where did you go?" She knew how he hated not knowing her every movement. It must have made him crazy to have her out of his control. "I went to an abbey. I needed to be quiet, to think, to try and see where we are going because, honestly, this last year has been exhausting, Nacho. I don't know that you understand any better than before what the problem is." "Well, you're not happy and I don't know why. You spend thousands of dollars every month you..." "Wait. Do you think that money is the problem?" "Well, it is a problem. I mean, you use the credit card until it's worn out." "This isn't about money, Nacho. I didn't go and spend three days alone at an abbey because I have issues with money." "What do you want?" "I want to be happy. I want you to share in our marriage. I feel like it's always me dragging you along. I want to feel like you are proud of my efforts at school, with the business. You hardly ever have time to spend with me, and I don't want to feel like I have the Gestapo watching over me every time I go out. I want to feel that you love me without fighting for it every inch of the way. I don't want a million dollars to be happy." "Yeah, right. Everyone would like a million dollars." "Would you rather lose a million dollars, or me, Nacho?" "I would rather lose you." "Do you know what you just said?" She was deadly calm. "Of course." "Do you mean it? Do you know what you're saying?" "Yeah. I said that I would rather lose you than a million dollars." He wasn't cocky, he wasn't angry. He was just stating a fact. "Nacho, I'm going to write down what you said." She reached over the desk and grabbed a note pad. She wrote, "I would rather lose you than lose a million dollars," and dated it. "Read it and tell me if this is what you really want to say. There's no misunderstanding." "No. There's no misunderstanding. That's what I meant," and he signed his signature with a flourish. "I'm saving this Nacho. This is a moment I will not forget, and when you do, I will have this piece of paper to remind you of what you lost today." But Angela left Chilo a month later and everything changed.

You can win, for a time, through ruthlessness and stealth; you can acquire more worldly goods than you will need, by sheer force and shrewd strategy... but sooner or later you will come to that point in your life when you will feel the pangs of remorse and the emptiness of your well-filled purse.

This year she had begun a course at the business school, in the entrepreneurship program, and had learned that there were many elements that each partner contributed to a business venture. The "angel" or "venture capitalist" contributed financial equity. Most start up companies or business propositions were cash poor; they looked for someone to "invest" in them. The smart investor looked for a business plan that had a highly viable idea that would bring him a tidy profit for his capital investment. The investor didn't spend his time coming up with ideas; the ideas worked for him and increased his net worth. She saw the correlation between the business arrangement and the marriage arrangement perfectly clearly. A marriage and a family couldn't survive on money alone, just as a relationship couldn't, just as a business couldn't; all needed many ingredients to make them successful, and a marriage, when it was reduced to value for input, value for investment per time, needed financial appraisal. Who had had the idea of what the marriage, home and a family were going to be like and put in the effort to sustain the venture? Who had put in more effort? Who had the concept? Who was the crucial link in the chain? Had one had more input and contributed more effort and time to the success of those ventures, or had it been an equal contribution? If one had been more prolific than the other in their contributions, then what was the value of that contribution? If one or both had contributed financially, then what was the equity value after twenty-three years of financial investment? A marriage, a relationship, had become reduced to nothing but money. But money wasn't an issue.

> **The "materialist doctrine" is the tendency to judge a person and their life, not by what they are or what they do, but by what they own.**

When she had decided to have her graduation party, she had gone to see Nacho at the office, where they could have privacy, to say, "Nacho, considering that you weren't supportive of my going to school, not even financially, I think that those that know this might find it strange that you would be there to celebrate my graduation. I think that it would be less stressful if you could find something else to do that day. The people that I have invited are my friends, my classmates, my co-workers from my business, not just acquaintances with the right kind of bank accounts or social connections. These people don't know how I live, what I have, or where I come from; they don't care "who" I am, but, "what" I am. They're here because they like me, just me, and what I can do. I didn't need *that* to get their respect," she added as she pointed to his father's portrait hanging behind him. "Well, maybe you could help me learn that," he said. "I'm sorry, Nacho, I tried, but you don't really want to be taught. You are what you are and so am I."

When she had graduated from university two weeks later, her parents had come to her graduation. At first, they had said that they wouldn't be coming, that they were tired, that it was hot in Tucson, that she didn't mind did she? She had been upset. She had thought that they would be proud to participate in the event with her. They had built their home in Vancouver next to the university gates so as to make the route to school as easy as possible for their daughters and had been so disappointed when she hadn't finished university, but married Nacho instead at the age of twenty. She had thought that they would have been mad with excitement to see her finally graduate, and with honours, but they seemed less than enthusiastic. She went to her thesis reading with her friend Bianca and to her Honours reception alone. One week before her graduation, her parents told her that they were coming. Her mother said, "We're coming." "We who?" she had replied. "Your father and I." "Since when did Dad say he was coming?" "He just decided. Besides, how many people did you send invitations to for your graduation? You shouldn't have done that. People will feel obliged to buy you a gift." "You mean like I did when they got married, graduated or had children?" "Don't be silly, it's not the same thing. You're old now." "You mean that if my cousins Steven or Andy had graduated from some course at this point in their lives, for the first time, it would not be a big deal? Or would it be a bigger deal because it would increase their earning potential as men? As the providers for their families, I mean. As far as that goes, I don't see anyone making a big deal of the fact that your sister's daughter Tina is working, being a mother, wife and housekeeper and going for her doctorate at the same time. Imagine if one of my male cousins was doing that. He would be deified." "Don't be silly. You are always angry. Every time I talk to you you're upset. What's wrong with you? How are the kids? I can imagine if you're busy with graduation and upset with what's going on, how that is affecting them." "Why don't you call me back, Mom, when you know when you're arriving?"

To be nobody but yourself— in a world that is doing its best night and day, to make you everybody else— means to fight the hardest battle which any human being can fight, and never stop fighting.

Nacho had not come to her graduation. Her mother, her father, Thano, Nicholas, Natascha, nephew Costa, her friend Bianca, who had incited her to go back to school, they were there because they wanted to applaud her efforts. Thano took a video as though he were the proud parent, Bianca beamed with pride, but her parents seemed distracted, as though they were there because they were supposed to be there, not because they wanted to be there. Her father was hot, harried and ready to go. He was physically there, had made the effort to come, but it felt the same as though he weren't present. The whole occasion felt devalued, because she could feel how little it mattered to him what she had accomplished. Her mother kept excusing him; he was tired, he was hot, he hadn't eaten. Her mom and dad were staying at the house in Tucson, so she drove down to Nogales that night after the ceremony to get everything ready for the party the next day.

If you use your brain, it's bound to create a problem for others if they are seeking to use, abuse, or control you, or keep you dependent or fearful.

The boys also went to Nogales to be there with her and help her prepare. They were already instinctively filling in for the absent husband in her life. She had planned the party while finishing her thesis, writing finals, meeting with Nacho and their lawyers to hammer out a divorce settlement, writing final papers, going to graduation luncheons, preparing for her thesis reading, attending her honours ceremony and readying the townhouse for her parent's arrival and weeklong visit. She had wanted the party to be a celebration of three years of successful hard work. She had wanted the party to bring together the disparate worlds that she had occupied until now— the social and personal friends from Tucson and Nogales, the academic, from the university, with her fellow students and professors, plus the design professionals and people who had helped her create her business. She wanted to bring together all the people who had participated in her journey, helping her find her way out of the world she didn't belong into a world where she did. She had hosted many parties over the years, usually at Christmas and on birthdays for her family, for Nacho, for the children, for her father, but she had never had one for herself in all that time, and now she wanted to celebrate and make up for all the celebrations she hadn't had. She wanted to have a party, even if no one had done it for her, and had planned with anticipation that it would be a happy and satisfying day. She hadn't foreseen that the other situations had been extensions, demonstrations of her love to the others, a gift from herself to others. The act of giving had pervaded every stage, from the food and music to the company's comfort and conversation. The party should have been a gift given to her this time, not of her, to herself. As her parents would later say, "How conceited, what an ego to give yourself a party. Who do you think you are?" not knowing that it dug into her like a dagger to be reminded that no one had done it for her.

As she, the boys, and Natascha went about the house getting ready for the party, she didn't feel the joy or anticipation as she had thought there would be. It felt sad. She walked through each room as though it were a last farewell, seeing what she had composed with such passion and determination as though it were a tomb she had placed herself in, deluding herself with beauty and with all that could solace her eye, proving to herself, to her family, to society, that this was enough to make herself, to make anyone, happy. At least content. But she now knew that without growth, freedom and without healing, the soul begins to shrivel up from lack of nourishment.

Her soul had been close to death. She had never thought until now that the face on the entry door, that of Demeter, was not just that of the earth mother, but the mother of Persephone, the young, beautiful woman kidnapped by Pluto and locked away in Hades in the underworld, her every exit and entrance, her life in the dark, owned and controlled by Pluto. This house had been both her salvation and her curse, allowing her to stay and survive as long as she had.

> **Those that do wrong... when there is no reason to do so, are the ones who persevere to the point of destruction.**

The night before the party, soon after they arrived in Nogales, she had found Thano in the living room, in the dark, with just the fireplace flickering as he sat on the sofa and gazed at the dance of the flames. He had looked so depressed. As she sat down next to him, she asked lightly, "What's up?" "I don't know, Mom. It just feels bad. Maybe this is the last time we're going to do this. This is our home and that's our crest over the fireplace. It feels weird that Dad's not here, Stephanie's not here. The house feels empty, like it's missing something." "Is that how you feel, Thano? I'm sorry. I wanted this to be a happy event and it feels like it's anything but that." Thano started to cry. He had been angry, he had distanced himself from her, he had been dejected as well, but now the tears had come. "I'm sorry, Mom. I'm so sorry, but it hurts so much when I think of all the times I saw you being so sad. It hurt me to see you unhappy. He can't help it, Mom. My dad is a very unhappy man, and he takes it out on you. That's all. He doesn't mean it, he really doesn't mean it." She had thought she was doing the right thing by trying to make it work no matter what the personal cost, but the cost had been more than personal, the cost had affected her children, the very ones she had tried to protect. As she held her grown son in her arms and tried to comfort him, she understood that the serenity prayer she had hung next to her vanity, next to the engraving of two little boys and a girl playing in the grass, had been strained through her own filter so that she couldn't really grasp the meaning of the words until now. "God grant me the serenity to accept the things I cannot change, the courage to change the things I can and the wisdom to know the difference." She had deleted all of it except for, "the courage to change the things I can," and had taken those things to be everything. She had grasped the determination and "the courage" to make anything work. How arrogant, how blind;

what a victim she had made of herself. But she had made them victims of her decision as well. She was a mother. She couldn't have felt worse as she felt her grown son cry, his tears wetting her blouse.

Why's pain the only way to happiness?

The next morning was busy as they readied the house for the guests who would arrive by noon. They were busy, but Thano, Nicholas and she were followed by shadows, shadows of what had been. The house was pristine and dressed for its guests with vasefulls of fresh flowers on the tables and the fountain splashing in the atrium. Pillows were fluffed, bedrooms tidy and the umbrellas on the terrace shone brightly in the sunshine as the open French doors invited the ubiquitous breeze that flowed in over the hills to come inside. Guests began to arrive, and it felt strange to have her friends from university, who had only known her for what she was intellectually capable of, to see her in a space that was such a personal expression of herself. It was also a very material reflection of her world, and for those that had only seen her on campus and in the classroom, it changed "what" she was to "who" she was. The carpenters, painters and other craftspeople were curious and satisfied to see what their work looked like when enhanced by an environment that was its complement. Even as she greeted her friends and showed them about, she felt wounded. It wasn't a happy day. It didn't feel like a celebration of successful endeavour, but an acknowledgment of failure. Her failure. She hadn't been able to keep this a house, this entity, this house of many faces, a home.

There can be no victory without loss.

Her parents arrived when the house was already full of guests, while she was conversing with the different groups. They looked upset. She heard her mother on the phone with Angela and when she got off, she looked as though she had been crying. Several people asked her if her parents were all right. She could feel their pain. She was leaving behind this home that was everything they had dreamed of for her. How many times had they brought relatives on sightseeing tours to Nogales, just so that they could see her home? She had lived the dream that "they" wanted for her, she too, had been proud that she had what they wanted, but they were devastated that she had chosen to leave it. They felt like failures as well. What had they done wrong? Why didn't she want what they wanted? Early in the afternoon they left, not staying until the end to help her clean up, as her mother usually did.

At one time in the counseling, when the therapist had begun to uncover the importance of the house to the family, he hadn't been able to make sense of her as he knew her, and this house that was, amongst other things, such an overt status symbol. "Why the house?" he had asked her. She was nonplussed, not having yet unraveled her complex, creative journey through the home to her own anagnorisis. "Why the house?" he repeated. She instinctively replied, "It was for my parents. For my mom and dad. The house was for them." Her house was her measure of success to them. In the Greek culture, the home was everything, and she was required to accomplish that for them, to make them proud, to prove that she had a good life.

A society that equates success with material acquisition, status and stability.

The day after, the boys left and she cleaned up and got ready to start school again the following day, starting pre-session with the classes she needed to finish off her degree requirements. Pre-session classes were brutally long and she was taking two a day. She had been on a mission to finish her degree so that she could move on with her life. But it was taking its toll, especially because she was emotionally drained from the constant sense of loss that enveloped her. Worse, and more deadly to her seemingly unquenchable spirit, was that she wasn't there for the love of learning anymore, but to commodify herself yet again with a piece of paper that would increase her value in one more dimension. After classes, she drove to the apartment that had been her refuge for the last two months. As soon as her parents had arrived, it had ceased to be her refuge and had become their home. For someone like herself, whose environment was so crucial to her personal energy, she was bereft, homeless, belonging neither in Nogales, nor there, not a wife, not yet a single woman, not self-sufficient, yet not reliant, a mother, yet without dependent children, a student, but with a "useless" degree she couldn't even get a job with. She was a designer, but one who had abandoned her dreams and the world she had created, removed herself from it by self-inflicted surgery. She felt so lost, tired and hopeless when she got to the apartment, and from her mother's reaction when she opened the door, she imagined her that she looked as bad as she felt.

It is better to die on your feet than to live on your knees.

"I have to lie down, Mom. Would you mind keeping the TV low? I really need to sleep." Her mother knew her daughter never napped and hardly slept. She looked alarmed. When she got up later her mother was waiting for her. She pounced. "What are you doing to yourself! Look at you! You're exhausted. Why did you go back to school? Why don't you take a break?" "Because I want to finish. Because I have to finish to get on with my life." "You're being selfish. Your children are going to hate you for this, what you have done to them, destroying their family. First school and now the divorce. All you think of is yourself." She thought of the years of torture trying to survive with a person so incompatible to herself, she thought of how she had finally seen the life she lived was the lesson she taught her children, that the life her mother had lived had taught her as well. Believing her role model to be perfect was in great part why she was here. "Look, Mom, your world revolves around Daddy and what he wants. That is and was your choice. It is not mine. Let me live my own life." Her mother almost howled with pain. This was the child who was her continuity, the one that she had showed off to the world as her personal trophy, the one who had it all, was it all, lived it all, the one who had what she could never be. She had to keep it. "I can't believe you. You are destroying everything." "I'm destroying what you want for me, Mom, not what I want. I'm working for what I want."

> **My love's more ponderous than my tongue.**

"Like your graduation invitations. You had to send them to everyone in Vancouver, all of our relatives. Who do you think that you are, showing off like that?" She was wounded that her mother could misperceive her genuine joy, and her need to share her accomplishment with those she felt to genuinely love her as false pride. "Stop it, Mom. Stop it before this goes too far. You do not control me. I will send graduation invitations if I want to. It is my life and it is my choice. I'm an adult and I don't need to ask your permission." "You see! You think that you are such a big shot now." "All I know, Mom, is that I don't need to listen to anyone who is trying to hurt me, and right now, ironically, that person is you." "Don't use your big words with me, trying to show off how smart you are." By now they were in the kitchen, voices raised, and her father boomed, "You think that you are something special because you got a degree now? All these people have filled your head with ideas that you can be a lawyer or a psychologist or a whatever. I have experience that you will never have. I am seventy-seven years old and you don't listen to me anymore. You know everything. You are so arrogant, you think that a piece of paper, or two, are going to give you anything close to what Nacho can provide you with? You are throwing everything away that people dream of their whole life long because of your big head. You want everyone to know how smart you are, sending them graduation invitations and announcements and giving yourself a graduation party to show off to all your new hippie friends what you have. You are selfish and inconsiderate beyond belief."

> **When the rash mood is on.**

She knew that at the core they were afraid that she couldn't look after herself. Their fear that she would be financially destitute without them, as Angela was, drove them to this cruelty, yet, they had taken Angela in and helped her, whether they resented it or not. They had helped Angela. "You want me to sell myself to Nacho, is that it? No matter what he is, no matter what my life is like, if I'm happy or not, you don't care as long as he pays for everything. Is that it? I don't need to listen to this. You gave me this house, you said it was mine; well you are offending me beyond what's acceptable. You need to go." She walked out, put on her shoes and left, crying as though her heart were being ripped out. She later found out that they had called Bianca to take them to the airport, distraught that their daughter could say such things to them. Two days later her father was hospitalized from the stress.

> **Such is life, it is often our best friends who throw us down.**

Angela, Nacho and her children would all find out about this scene and saw what had happened as a complete loss of respect for her elders. Angela and Nacho would rub it in forever, saying what an ungrateful and cruel daughter she had been, how she had hurt her parents when they had spent thousands of dollars to come to her graduation and show their support.

> **To question the customs and laws of marriage is to question society itself, its distribution of money, power and love.**

She could understand what they didn't or couldn't, that she was fighting a value system her parents had brought from Greece with them and never abandoned: girls don't flaunt their intelligence, don't talk back to their elders, even in self defense. She knew that the culture she lived in, both Greek and Mexican, valued sympathy, unselfishness, loyalty, purity, a quiet muffled voice and obsequious nature in a female, conceding dominance to the males who surrounded and controlled her. These males would then maintain her, first, her father, then a husband, as was appropriate, as she was the weaker, defenseless, sex. She was owned, maintained, bartered, as surely as though married off with a dowry, her life exchanged for money, a house, a car, jewelry, vacations. In that value system, her worth was reduced to... money.

> **In a patriarchal culture, mothers are blamed for the pain their children experience in trying to fit the narrow roles that the culture demands. Mother blaming directs the energy towards hunting down the wicked witch so that we pay no attention to the man behind it all.**

She looked away from the copperplate engraving and sat back in her chair, turning to look out the French doors toward the sunlight and green plants outside. She had always looked to the outdoors, where she was just another creature moving through her time on earth, as a reality check, to keep things in perspective. All the things inside these walls, and even the walls themselves, had distorted reality in such a destructive way. The only thing that had remained real was the love she had felt for Nacho for so many years, the love for her children that was still immeasurable and the love for her parents that would somehow survive hard words and hurt feelings. That love had been so much a part of the beauty she had created. It couldn't have been what it was otherwise; it showed in every nuance of the world she built, because her work was for the love of creation, not from the need for possession. That was why money didn't erode her. It didn't feed her soul; beauty and love did.

> **For the world of man is not only a world of things; it is a world of symbols where the distinction between reality and make believe is itself unreal.**

Chapter SEVENTEEN

THE BODY

She glanced at herself in the mirror as she walked into the gym, her image interrupted in the floor-to-ceiling mirror by the chrome equipment that gleamed in the overhead light. She was here to work, work with her body, work to make it strong, work, so that this vehicle that carried the essence of her where she wanted to go carried her efficiently. Even though she was highly conscious of the fact that she lived in a world of images where she and everyone else was judged by their appearance, she was here to work so that she could age with grace, so that her muscles would respond when she needed them, work so that her bones would be strong when she was old and work so that she could run when she wanted, walk where she wanted and live a physically full life.

The blood around men's hearts is their thought.

She wanted to make sure that she had taken care of the vessel whose every function was a reflection upon her life. Most importantly, she was here to create a stronger symbiotic relationship between her body and her mind so that the strength in her muscles came into balance with strength of purpose, strength of character. When she felt physically strong, she had more energy, more power; it was like she was carrying extra voltage, electrifying those around her with her personal aura, feeding off of herself.

> **The body is... a point of view and a point of departure.**

She needed to be strong to break free of the traditions and customs, the insecurities and the patterns of the old life she had known and to move on to the new one she wanted to create. She needed a lot of strength to start a new life built with the strength of truth, the strength of knowledge and the strength of self respect. She had read that when you smile, your mind responds as though it is truly happier, even though the emotion is simulated. She saw the correlation, that by forcing her body to be stronger, by convincing herself that she could do it, she would create her reality, reach her destination.

> **It is an unvarying law of nature that strength grows out of resistance.**

She needed physical exercise as much as she needed mental exercise. She turned on the treadmill and stepped onto the revolving band, determined to give herself the physical exercise she needed, the exercise she needed to grow stronger, to tire herself enough to sleep because she had so much natural energy that she often ran instead of walked just to burn it off. She needed the intellectual exercise because her mind was insatiably curious, always seeking, learning, growing. She knew them to be intrinsically intertwined, interdependent— exercise for the mind and the body were there to develop and empower herself.

> **Man is of soul and body formed for deeds**
> **Of high resolve; on fancy's highest wing**
> **To soar unwearied, fearlessly to turn**

The machinery was there to serve her, strengthen her, empower her; it was composed of steel, as though the very substance of the material would align itself with her body to withstand abuse. She looked in the mirror and saw...

herself. She didn't see what others saw, but the vessel made of flesh and bone that housed her mind and soul. Her eyes looked outward, she only saw herself in the mirror for a few minutes at a time, glimpses of what others could study and observe. She remembered reading *Gulliver's Travels*, and how, in it, the change in body size had everything to do with looking at the body in a new perspective, the corporeal perspective rather than the social or spiritual.

These hidden beauties are commonly by far the greatest, because the more complex a beauty is, the more hidden is it.

She knew that she wasn't just a body, even though it had taken her so long to get past what others insisted on defining as her best asset. Even now she bristled to hear, "You're attractive, you'll remarry," as though that was the best thing she had in her favour. From the time she could remember as a child it was, "Look at what pretty eyes she has. Look at what pretty hair. She has such a nice figure. You have nice feet. I love your nose. It's because you have a heart shaped face. You have nice legs. I like your behind. What great eyebrows. Look at your cupid bow mouth. I like your widow's peak." Parts. Parts. Parts. Pieces of her that could be seen as parts of a composition, parts that were pleasing to their eyes. Did they really see her at all? What did they see when they looked at her? Because she didn't feel as though they really saw *her*. She fought to define herself on her own terms so as not to lose the ability to live freely and powerfully in her own body, claiming her power through it. If she didn't, she would allow others to dehumanize and disempower her. The young man in a wheel chair, the young woman with cystic acne, the child without an arm, the young boy forty pounds overweight, the woman that was "too black," she often could see it in their eyes. They wanted to be seen for who they were, not what they looked like.

She often felt at peril, living with the issue of female sexuality in a culture shaped by androcentrism, one where deep feeling was often split from physical sensation, leaving her to survive in a culture where a woman's body was reduced to a source of sensation and pleasure. Sensory. A person who was dehumanized, hunted, game. That was the attraction of voyeurism, of the objectification, of looking at and not connecting with anyone in a real way, paying for the use of a body, or just using a body, by getting together for a few minutes or a few hours. That's what they wanted from her. That way there was no commitment on any level, no intimacy. It was reduced to an act. Many didn't want to see that this value system often converged with that of traditional "committed" relationships, one she had lived as well, that it happened with or without a wedding ring over and over again and often to the very same people that sat in judgement of others. The body lost the gift for human intimacy and became just a body. She was then, just a body. She defied Nacho's or anybody else's invasion of her right to be herself.

> **She appears essentially to the male as a sexual being... she is defined and differentiated with reference to man and not he with reference to her.**

Even though she described herself as a "postmodern agnostic," she was sensitive to a sense of spirit, soul, and the tremendous power that it wielded. When she had seen someone die, the body everyone recognized remained, and yet, the person ceased to exist. The corporeal contained the spirit, and the spirit, the soul. It was the far more important of the two entities, yet it was intangible, and by being intangible, less valued. Things that were intangible were difficult to give a value to; material things were far easier to appreciate. She saw the rampant objectification of women, the era of the "supermodel," as a world she had seen evolve in the last twenty years with the proliferation of strip clubs, swinger groups and women in the media arts as billboard draws, video game draws, porno site draws. Bodies had become icons. Elle, Pamela Anderson, faces had become icons, Cindy Crawford, Drew Barrymore and their iconisisem had evolved because of the value society placed upon women's appearance, not their abilities or souls. She saw no parallel in the world of the male in the human species. Yes, men were esteemed and valued as being more sexually desirable because of their appearance, but not to the same degree. Men created their value through their work, much more so than women. She saw that reality and lived with that reality every day as a member of her sex. It was her need to be respected as more than a human specimen of a body that made her complicated. She couldn't and didn't want to make a trade, using her appearance as her calling card, and resented any woman who was devalued by that same system. Her thoughts, her imagination, her spirit, her instincts, her needs, were things contained in this vessel which carried her around, this vessel which was the most invaluable asset because it housed her, not because of its appearance, but because it was where she lived. Because of her appearance, like those with a physical defect or handicap whose physicality dominated their space in the world, she was a person defined by society from the outside in rather than from the inside out.

She remembered standing at the bedside of her beloved, dying uncle in the hospital just a few months ago. She had been standing near his head and could hear the air coming in and out of the corrugated, plastic pipe that went into his mouth. The air made more noise passing through the plastic than it did through soft, moist, human, tissue and it seemed as though the noise made it visible, as though she could actually see the vapor feeding his body. The monitor above his head had marked his breathing, marked the rhythm of his lungs just as the rhythm of his lungs were tied to that of his heart. She had been so conscious of the fact that the air was what sustained his life. The artificiality of the loud breathing, because the air was being forced into him by a machine, wasn't comforting, but intrusive, unnatural. The machine was keeping his body alive when the body knew that its work was done.

> **It is tasteless to prolong life artificially... it is time to go.**

He had been fighting death for most of his life. When a young man in his early thirties, a young man with four children under the age of five, he was diagnosed with a rare illness, lupus. He had beat the odds over and over again, outlasting two kidney transplants and two heart attacks to come back to life again and again, determined to live so that he could take care of his family and see them grow up. The doctors often said that it was sheer will which kept him going, that there was no medical explanation as to how his body still functioned with all that it had gone through... Even unconscious, his will was formidable.

> **Will is of all possible concepts the only one that has its origin not in the phenomenon, not in the mere representation of perception, but which comes from within.**

The time came for his body to finally defeat his will. His body had had enough even though his spirit kept fighting to defy the odds yet again. Now he was unconscious. It wasn't him. It was the body that his family and loved ones gathered around.

> **As a heavenly breath which animates the body.**

Finally the lines on the monitor, marking his life, became a flat line, then the line disappeared as well and letters replaced the body rhythms to write textual data: a name, a birth date, a death date. The time of death. The time he ceased to be because the machine wasn't enough to keep him alive. His soul was done, his will was done and so, the body was no longer working; it no longer housed the man. Death had seemed so unnatural. It shouldn't have been like this, with a machine to validate his existence and cessation of existence. Where was he that a machine could measure, what had he been that a machine could value? Ah. But the body was what mattered to the machine. Not the man, not the will. The body was what mattered to the nurses and doctors, the professionals, the funeral director. Sons, daughters, wife, family, friends, they wanted the man back, not the body. The body was still there.

As any tombstone was an illusion of permanence for a body that decayed and disappeared, it was right and fair that a life well lived was the far more enduring legacy. She had seen again that a life worth living was not about monuments, wealth or beauty, but about living with personal integrity. Anyone who taught "good things" by example left a legacy of a life worthy of recognition and admiration. That was what fostered the love and respect when a soul left and the body remained, when the least valuable part, the body, the empty house, was all that was left. That was what monuments were built for, human beings with extraordinary spirit. The bodies made the spirit possible.

> **Spiritual beauties are infinitely the greatest, bodies being but the shadows of beings.**

◆ ◆ ◆

There had been a series of milestones she had mentally faced in order to build up her strength enough to break free of Nacho. One of the biggest confrontations had been about her going to a gym in Vancouver while she had lived there, that summer in 2000. She had felt a need to build up her strength that, in hindsight, was almost eerie. Just like other creatures know when it is time to hibernate, fly south or hide from danger, she had known somehow that to break free, she needed to be strong. Very strong.

> **The athlete whose muscles been formed by exercise is a joy to the eye, but he is also better fitted for the contests in which he must engage.**

When Nacho had arrived from Nogales and found out that she was going to a gym at six in the morning, he had been apoplectic. "You can't go to the gym at six," he had said, "Go later." "I don't want to go later, then my whole morning is shot. I want to go early and get it over with so that I have the rest of the day free for Stephanie or whatever else I want to do." "That's when all the men go, before they go to the office. Go later when there are just women there." "No. I don't want to go later. I don't care if men are there and anyhow, there aren't just men at that time, there are women as well. My trainer is a woman too and she doesn't care if men are in the gym. Imagine. She would have to shut down if she didn't want men to see her in her work out clothes." "You just want to go at that time because you like all the men to look at you. You want them to look at you."

Is the body useful or beautiful? The two are intertwined. The two are so closely intertwined as to be almost identical.

"You're always making me out to be someone I'm not. You're not going to lock me up like one of your women from Culiacan. I'm not ashamed of my body. As far as I know, everybody has one. I'm not going to be locked up so that nobody can look at me. Women here go to the gym when they like, where they like, and I am too. We don't live by your rules here." "You will live by my rules. You're not going to the gym in the morning." "I will do what I like and if I want to go to the gym in the morning, or at noon or at night, that's my decision, not yours. You don't own me. I'm your wife, not a body that you own and control. I'm a human being and I have the right to live my life, my way, making my own choices. You're not going to make them for me." He was furious, and so was she. There was no meeting ground. He hated that he couldn't control her, and she was so tired of his looking for the worst to happen, always expecting the worst from people, even from her, even though he knew that she had never betrayed, lied to or cheated him.

All oppression creates a state of war.

As she faced the mirror, she could see what others saw, that even now her body was trim. People judged her because of her body, because of her face, just as they judged others by the same yardstick. She remembered being at a meeting with Nacho a year before as they tried to repair the damage to their marriage. The group required that they not sit together, and she had been sitting next to a woman who was sweet, gentle, kind, very overweight and very self conscious about her weight. When the exercise given them to describe how they felt about their body began, the woman glanced at her sideways. "Oh," the woman had sighed, "I had hoped that I wouldn't be sitting next to someone who was slim when we had to do this. It makes it so difficult for me." "I know. I have a sister who has battled with her weight ever since she was nine and I was six. I know that's how she feels every time she sees me as well, and there's nothing I can do about it. Just by being the way I am, I make her feel bad and I know it. It hurts her and it hurts me." "Oh, I'm sorry. I didn't think that you would understand."

> Differences and melodies of the living, human, body.

And it happened all the time. Even her mother would apologize saying, "You must think I'm ugly, I'm so fat," as though assuming that she would be judgmental regarding those who weren't like her. She remembered when she had had Thano, her firstborn. She had just delivered him and the doctor had looked at her lying on the delivery table, waiting for the nurses to clean, weigh and measure her baby, and said, "You are going to be hated by women the world over." She hadn't understood what he was talking about, but the comment had seemed so strange that it had stuck in her mind. She had later realized after visiting many friends with their own newborns, that she was lucky, just lucky, that her body snapped back to shape as though she had never had a baby.

> "Too good looking."
>
> ♦
>
> "She'll be married soon."
>
> ♦
>
> "She's the kind you want to marry."

For so many women it was a struggle, women who felt themselves less than what they wanted to be because of their body image, because they felt judged, because of what their bodies looked like, not because of who they were. To many, a female that didn't have to work hard to have a nice body had an unfair advantage. That was different, and different was, of course, for many, unfair or bad. The mistress of studies when she was in grade eleven at the Convent, had been upset with her because she had slacked off at school and dropped a couple of A's to B's, saying, "You're not going to get through life on your looks," as though she believed that she would forever belittle herself trying. She had unfairly assumed that any attractive female would take that route.

> **She has a sparkling intelligence, but despite her passionate nature, she is not attractive enough to represent a danger to anyone.**

Years later, it would be a young woman in her honours program, a fellow classmate and intellectual peer, who looked her up and down and said, "You don't need to be here. I do," disparaging her ability, her desire and need to learn as being less that her own because of the same superficial perception she had been judged by twenty-five years earlier.

In the world of Culiacan, a woman's primary role was as a mother and, secondarily, as wife. Her appearance, her body, were hugely, monumentally, important in a society that didn't expect women to do anything more productive than give birth, a society that didn't validate female strength or spirit, confining them to a life of dependency. That society had tried to confine her to that definition of what a female was as well. She had often seen the faces, heard the comments, which belittled her efforts with her business and her school because it made them uncomfortable. "A woman who abandons her responsibility in the home to waste her time with an unnecessary career, especially when she sacrifices the care of her husband and her children to do so, is destroying society itself," one woman had said when she was sure she would hear it.

> **The moment I treat my body as an object... I banish myself to infinity.**

Her son Thano wanted her to look and dress like a young stylish mother. He was proud of her appearance. Her middle child, Nicholas, wanted her to look like, and be, just "his mother," and Stephanie, her daughter, described her as "elegant," watching and learning about personal style through her. She was the same person and played the same role for all of them, but it was their own perceptions of her that were different. In a society that valued image over substance, whether in Canada, the United States, Europe, Asia or Mexico, an attractive image helped. As a daughter, her parents saw her as a fine showpiece, and as a wife, Nacho wanted her to be invisible. It was as though these people who loved her, each in their own way, saw their image as indelibly linked to hers. She just wanted to be herself, to be comfortable in her own skin.

Care for the limb, the thews, the stature, bulk, and big assemblance of a man! Give me the spirit.

Once, when they had left Nacho at his gate in the airport and were walking back to the car, she had asked Nicholas, "Do you like the way that I'm dressed, Nick?" Nicholas had said, "Yes, Mom, you always look nice." "Then why doesn't your father say so? I always feel like he disapproves or is criticizing?" "That's because you're nice looking, Mom, and when you dress nice as well, it attracts more attention— and Dad doesn't like that. It's not your fault and it's not a bad thing. Don't pay attention to him. I know that it upsets you, but its not you, it's him." Curiously, she had never felt sure of her "beauty" to Nacho, only her appeal, as though the two were disconnected. She had wanted Nacho's approval then and had wanted it for a long time, since forever it seemed. It didn't matter now. She had become strong enough that his approval, or anyone else's, wasn't how she measured her own worth. For the first time in her life, she understood how, by creating so many beautiful things that others could possess, she had subconsciously de-objectified herself. No one would ever own her again. Only the things she created were for sale, not herself.

As for her, she used herself as a mannequin on which proportion, color and texture were all materials to play with in a creative combination of design elements. It wasn't about an outward status statement. It was for her a manifestation of her spirit. Others judged her for that as well, just as she saw the woman with tattoos and black leather biker clothes and assumed certain things about her. Nacho had tried to control what she wore from the beginning, treating her as his own mannequin, making a statement about who he was instead of allowing her to be herself. He had fought to create the social image he wanted her to portray by erasing who she was. She had fought to defy that control, learned to overcome her insecurity and finally come to enjoy the power of who she was, not just what she was. It had taken her years to understand and overcome why he valued her. Years, and it had almost destroyed her to be married to a man who couldn't understand or communicate with her as a person, only as someone he was physically attracted to. His private toy. His body.

In another class she had taken with a group of women ranging in age from eighteen to seventy, a very pretty young woman had spoken of her objectification, of how her husband loved to dress her up and show her off to his friends with form fitting dresses. "How do you feel?" someone had asked her. "How does it feel when he does that?" Her face had crumpled and tears had dripped down her cheeks as she whispered, "Ashamed." Every woman in the group who had ever felt herself used by her man as a projection of his own status felt that woman's pain as a part of her own.

She had come to her own conclusion— that men who valued their wives primarily for their appearance were going to be easily attracted to and distracted by any other female that they found attractive as well. If appearance was what they sought first, a woman was just a shape to them. A body. A face. A status symbol. "You're not going to wear that are you? Have you gained weight? What did you do to your hair? You're wearing too much makeup. What's that on your eyes? I'm not going out with you in that outfit. If you don't change, we're staying home."

Even the therapist, a man, had openly condemned other therapists, fathers, friends, those who abused their positions of authority to hurt women, constantly commenting on their unethical behaviour, had betrayed her trust. Dishonorable. Disgusting. Dishonest. She had trusted this man to take care of her as she had trusted Nacho, her husband, to take care of her, to care about *her*. But they had sacrificed her well being for their own desires, sacrificed her because they couldn't overcome their own insecurities instead, using her for compensation. Using her.

His reputation had entitled him to trust by association because he worked out of a prestigious clinic that drew clients from Europe and all over the continent. His betrayal had rocked her. She had finally learned to open up and trust someone with her innermost thoughts, to speak of the shame of living a reality so different than the image that people assumed to be real. She had trusted him to empower her, to believe and support her in this time of transition, to help her grow, to see her as a person, complex and complete. She had trusted him to protect her from Nacho, to teach Nacho, help her children. Instead of taking care of her, he had almost destroyed her faith in herself, in her intuition, in her own ability to read people and situations that were a threat.

I've got a hole in me now
I've got a scar I can talk about.

He had damaged her natural self-defense system, a system created by her body and her mind to protect her from harm. She had been manipulated by someone who knew how to play with human needs and weaknesses. But she had not been a victim. Even though the betrayal had left her feeling adrift, incompetent and vulnerable as she sought to understand what he and Nacho had wanted from her, unable to separate the betrayal of one from the other, she had finally found peace and strength, had been able to accept that the problem wasn't her.

Resolve to be thyself: and know that she who finds herself, loses her misery.

She had fought so hard to be so much more. More than a body. But they had liked what they saw more than what she was. It wouldn't have happened otherwise, so, in a way, it was her fault. She had provoked it. She had deserved it. Just like she deserved the guy in the ultralight who had turned off the engine to get her to go out with him, just like she deserved her friend's father trying to kiss her on the mouth when he helped her put her two small boys in the car, just like she deserved her son's friend telling him his mother was "hot," as though she were a bitch in heat, just like she deserved the boys in high school who had turned off the lights at a party to grab her in the dark, the man that wouldn't give her a drink if she didn't pony up a kiss, her husband's cousin leering at her like a stalker every time he was in her company, the "gentleman" who walked up to her at a friend's apartment saying, "I'm hung like a horse and it's my birthday. Do you want to give me a good time?" Wasn't that what Nacho said? That it was the way she dressed, that it was the way she looked, the way she talked, the way she smiled, because she was where she shouldn't be— because, because, because... it was always her fault. Of course they weren't going to see her as a person. That part of her wasn't valuable. She was a body.

It was when she learned to give it right back to them, believing that she owned herself, that she became strong and enjoyed the power of living in her own skin. That was when her world changed. She became stronger, her body her own in every sense.

We reclaim our ability to trust others as we reclaim trust in ourselves.

The discipline she exercised in looking after her body was about housekeeping. It was where she lived, and her ancestors, the ancient Greeks, had been so wise in proposing that a healthy mind needed to be housed in a healthy body. She sometimes resented the amount of time it took from "her life" to care for it; to eat, wash it, groom it, cut hair, comb hair, cut nails, shave, put on makeup, exercise. Even though she savoured chocolate or warm, buttered toast with hot tea, she ate conscientiously. She chose wheat bread over white, tomato sauce over cream, bean soups over fried food, so as to nourish the body she lived in, rather than just fill it.

For awhile, she had used the food she ate as an emotional flood gate. When she was unhappy she ate chips, ice cream, a hamburger, french fries— food she wouldn't touch when she was "looking after herself." These were the foods that she could eat when she felt unhappy, to hurt herself when life felt out of control, when she didn't like who she was or where she was. She ate to compensate for her life just because she could. She knew these were luxuries she could have and waste because she had food and water to squander, just as many others did not. She knew, her mind told her, that she wasn't supposed to use food to compensate for a lack of personal power in her life. She needed to empower herself in a healthier way, by making her body and mind stronger so that she could fight back. Her instincts were innate, and she had learned to listen to them more carefully, without distraction. When she chose to exercise, go to school, run her business and make a life for herself outside of her home, her mind and spirit began to build strength and heal. She began to believe that she would find a life where she could be strong and free.

So integral to the healing of the body was the mind, that the god of medicine carried a staff with the symbols of both intertwined... the caduceus was the ancient symbol of body and soul.

Her father had told her stories of trapping small birds on the island, swimming off the rocks to catch fish and sea urchins in the crystalline Aegean Sea because he was hungry, because what they caught was all there was to eat. Both her parents had told her stories of living off of potatoes, almonds and dried figs for months because there was no other food. Finding food had taken up a great part of their lives, just in order to keep their bodies alive. That had been the beginning of her father's love of hunting and his obsession and passion for food. For her, gathering food was a luxury— time spent shopping and cooking because she wanted to, not because she had to, just as walking was a choice, not a necessity to get from one place to another. The basic human need to go out and gather food in order to sustain life had been deformed, changed to fit the needs of the world she lived in. The world her body lived in was a veritable cornucopia of plenty where people "chose" not to eat. The human body had developed with a purpose, just as the fish grew fins and birds, wings to sustain their life's purpose, so too her limbs needed work to be strong— as her mind needed work to fulfill its purpose. If she didn't give them work, they would atrophy and become soft and impotent. She defied the world of privilege that Nacho wanted to tie her to by giving herself the work she needed. She knew that, if she let it, the world of privilege would do nothing for her except make her weak. The body's beauty lay in its miraculous ability to function, every cell of it had a function, just as the miracle of the human mind lay in the strength and breadth and endlessness of it. Denying the beauty was its destruction.

> Good for the body is the work of the body.

She used her discipline and determination to encompass much more of her than her body. Her discipline encompassed honing character, drive, ambition, determination, foresight and insight as well, training her mind to build strength and help her survive. Those qualities were what athletes, scientists and physicians understood as the connection she intuitively fought for.

> Discipline is a means for solving life's problems.

Perhaps that was why the physical appearance of others had never been important to her. She was a humanist by nature, fascinated by the psyche, culture and habits that made each human a unique composition. She was a being who could create whole worlds that didn't yet exist in her mind, objects that didn't exist, people, music, dimensions that didn't really exist, but their very creation in her mind gave them the possibility to be real, tactile, lived with. Touched. The essence was what mattered, that which was untouchable, in her heart, mind and soul. Possibility was human, not bestial.

Some people were too busy with the world outside to look within; she was always acutely aware of both.

> Man's character is his fate.

Nacho had loved her being pregnant; it had been proof of his ownership and virility. His body in her, her belly proof that she was his. She had wanted each of her children as much as he had. Each was planned and a gift to herself and the world when they were born. To Nacho, it was his child, she, his vehicle. As in the days of slavery, a child born was property, his, his flesh and blood, as she never could be. His children would always be a part of him. Nacho was not a man to abandon his children. It was one of the things she had instinctively known about him, one of the things that had attracted her to him on the most primal level. She was part of him forever, marked a part of her, his, he implanted in her, possessing her in a way that could never be reciprocal. It was an attitude that she would experience time and time again, until she could finally assimilate it. To him her body was a vessel for procreation, and, on that most basic level, was the only reason for his, their, sexual attraction. That was why she was his, his mate and his alone. His continuity was through his children, the reason to work, his reason for creating an empire. Unlike other men she had seen, Nacho's children were his life, his purpose. He would always take care of them.

He would see that his child was well provided for. That was a father's duty.

Almost a year after Stephanie was born, she had thought that she was pregnant again. She had been panicked at the thought of carrying another baby, of another four to five months in bed, of having another child to bring up. "I don't want another child. My body is not just for making babies. I am not just a vessel. Three are enough. I want to do other things in a few years, not be tied down to pregnancy and childcare. I have wants and needs too." "What are you talking about? How can you even talk like that? Of course you'll have the baby if you're pregnant. I won't hear of anything else." They had battled for days. But she hadn't been pregnant. It had been another test, a test of herself as a woman, her test, Nacho's test, a test of their marriage. It had taught them things about one another and their belief systems that again proved how different they were. Her belief system assumed that her body was hers; he assumed that her body was theirs.

She had thought of the friend who had become unexpectedly pregnant with her fourth child when she thought she was done having children. She had been unhappily pregnant, and felt cursed when her little girl was born with learning disabilities. She remembered her friend from high school who had gone to Hawaii in grade ten, fifteen years old, and come home pregnant. Her life had been forever compromised and so, so, different from what she might have lived. She thought of another friend who had been treated for tumors on her ovaries, going through months of radiation in her late forties, only to find out at the end that she was thirty six weeks pregnant, just as she was ready to sign the contract for her dream job and send her youngest child off to junior high. She thought of the young woman in Culiacan, who had had carried her only child, born dead, in her body for nine months.

Her body. This vessel that contained her had defined her in so many ways from the day she was born— to her parents, to family, to friends at school, to her husband, the woman at the supermarket, the man on the street. As she slowed down to a walk, she looked at herself in the mirror, at the rivulets of sweat running down her face and chest. She felt strong, proud that she could do this for herself. She could choose to run if she wanted to move, she could use her body freely to take her wherever she wanted to go. She wasn't limited by her physique as to the life she could lead. Every part of her worked. She didn't even need glasses. She had never fought illness, had rarely even had a cold. Her skin took the sun well, she didn't fear sunburn, hadn't suffered from acne, didn't get stretch marks when she was pregnant, didn't need braces, she didn't have a heart condition, arthritis-lupus. She wasn't allergic to foods... God, she was lucky. So lucky. She looked in the mirror and saw... herself. This body that was her home, the home that she would take with her was strong, determined, self-sufficient and capable because her mind said it was so. Her body, her mind, were of this earth and were the gifts that gave her life and the ability to live it to the fullest. She could go forward and remake, rebuild, reward herself with a life built on her own terms because she had this body to do it with.

As she bent over, turned off the switch on the treadmill and stood up, she felt the power of possibility, the opening out of the potential she had to live and experience life. She had a good house to take with her, and she could use this gift to fulfill her potential. She was stronger now. Her body was finally ready for the journey. It was time to go.

To find joy and contentment in understanding how everything is connected.

Chapter EIGHTEEN

The Gate

Walking out of the exercise room, she shut the door. She had taken from it what she needed to move forward. And she did. She walked down the hall to her bedroom, past the bureau with the faces of her children, sister, mother, father, mother-in-law and, in the back, the black-and-white photo of Nacho's father. Serious, somber, he had done what he could to find the person to take care of Nacho when he was gone.

> Father's sorrow, father's joy.

He had taken her measure, knowing better than anyone else that she was the right woman for his son, that she would be able to survive the personal cost. She walked through the doorway through her bathroom to her closet and opened the door. She reached for her jacket and saw the box high on the shelf, the box with the flowery bathing suit still inside. She turned off the closet light, shut the door, and as she turned she glanced at the vanity drawer that still held the gold band with the single diamond set in the gold leaves and berries. Her eyes saw herself reflected in the mirror, the same mirror that had trapped her eyes last Christmas morning as she had looked at her face with the water and tears streaming down, feeling like the murderess of her family. She walked past the lithograph of the three children playing in the grass next to her vanity, past the serenity prayer she had hung there for inspiration. How could she have known that she would have to look at it for years and read it an infinite amount of times before being able to empower herself with its words of wisdom?

> **How good, how gainful, how happy it must needs be to live according to honesty and justice.**

She walked through the door, past the chair with its ghosts of gifts from Christmas Past, and looked at the bed, the bed she had shared with her husband, the bed that had felt like a trap, a compromise, a vise when she howled for hours and hours, fighting to find her way out of the world where she didn't belong. This was the bed where she had warmed her feet against his and felt him against her back, his arm over her in the dark, under the covers. This was the bed where she had lain for so many nights, alone, waiting for his steps in the hallway. Only they and the bed knew those moments.

She walked out of her room and passed the door to Stephanie's room. Her daughter's childhood photo looked out the door at her, the little girl gripping the back of the chair upon which she stood with determination and strength, the expression of determination, the grip of the little hands proof of character uncommon in one so young, her bright gaze prescient evidence of the keen mind she would grow into. She glanced across the hall, through the door into Nicholas' room. His photo looked out at her with the face of a child so happy he didn't see conflict or sorrow, just his own satisfaction with his place in the world. As was benefiting the second son, his place in their family was affirmed by two beds, two mirrors; his relationship to his older brother and sister was a profound, compelling and indelible part of him, as was his contentment proven in his kind nature. She continued a few steps and stood in the doorway to Thano's room, the room he had never really lived in except for brief periods, because it had been his time to go when they moved into the house. His photograph betrayed that he saw too much and that he always had. He gazed at her with thickly-lashed eyes that saw things beyond his years, burdened by her sadness. The burden of that perception had always weighed upon him, a weight that he still hadn't freed himself from.

We cannot be just if we are not kind hearted.

She turned and made her way through the tall, mirrored gates that could no longer hold her with the specters of times past, nor with the illusion of what might have been. They no longer trapped her. She moved through them down the steps to where the shadows of Nacho's and her fallen figures lay, his bone protruding from his leg, her body fighting to live, and she could let them go. They too were part of the past. She walked up the steps of the great room and stared at the chair where she had sat enjoying the flickering flames of the fire with the company of a good book, the candlesticks on the table. She gazed at the engraving of the two old men savouring the cache of gold that their eyes greedily, falsely, believed would bring them happiness, and then looked at the mirror above them, the mirror that reflected the other one in front of it. The twins of illusion and escape no longer served a purpose. She didn't need the mirrors for truth, escape or illusion any more.

Design is an apparent expression and declaration of the "concetto" that is held in the mind and that which... has been imagined in the intellect.

As she turned to walk into the kitchen, the gates that led down to the wine cellar formed a pretty pattern of wrought-iron against the cool, cream, plaster stairwell. She hoped that the journey down into that netherworld was one she never traveled again; she knew she had seen too much of that grim reality to be unaware of the destination.

As she walked into the kitchen, the aesthetic combination of the soft, constant light from the overhead skylights, the dark green and cream cabinets with their elegant cornice, the deep umber and cream checkerboard tiles and wrought-iron overhead light still evoked visual delight, even as the almost invisible pewter clock on the bookcase shelf took her back again to that moment when she had chosen change over this.

Food becomes blood, blood becomes heart and brain, thought and mind, stuff.

Change over what she had known in this home, inside these walls, change over what she had seen as a pattern her whole life long. That small, little ornament had begun the journey she was committed to once she began it. She hadn't known it then, but there had only been one possible destination for that evolutionary path, a path where she was her only companion, walking steadfastly where she needed to go alone. She walked through the soothing gloom of the dining room, through the stone portal of the living room and looked at the symmetry of her creation with a sadness that came and went as soon as it was acknowledged. She was no longer part of a pair, her mother's pillows weren't her destiny. They were part of her history. She wanted to take the memories of Nicholas' fingers stroking sweet melody from the keys of the piano in the corner, of friends and family talking, laughing over good conversation and company on the soft sofas, of Nacho lying with his feet up on the table while he took a nap in front of the fire, of Stephanie curled up on the sofa, absorbed in a book or on the phone with a friend, of Thano sitting on the other sofa with her, talking about where his life was and where he wanted it to go. This room belonged to all of them, not just to her image looking down from the wall, not just to her evolution as a woman, but to their evolution as a family, a unit that would contain all of them as long as they lived, and even when no one remained. They were their own history.

A genuine sense of mortality enables us to see virtue as the only thing of worth; and it is impossible to limit and foresee the ways in which it will be required of us.

But her portrait still had its story; it would always tell a story. Nicholas had said that it should never be taken down from its place on the wall, that she should always be a part of this work of art she had created— her face, her signature, her legacy. Unlike the portrait of the young woman on the other wall, in times to come, she would not be anonymous, the stone wall beneath her hand, carved with her name, would testify to the place she had occupied in the world, even when she ceased to be, a testimony of her life as a headstone never could be. Stephanie said that it was to be hers; that this portrait of her mother was her "patrimony." Earlier, when she and Nacho had walked through the house, deciding what belonged to whom, she had been taken aback when they came to this room with the portrait. "I don't suppose you want that anymore,

even though I gave it to you."
"Yes, I do," he had replied, "I do want it." It had been a poignant moment, clear to both of them that he now wanted this memento of what he had once had.

I will remember you. Will you remember me?

She turned to go down the steps and glanced up into the second floor of the study. She stepped in and, coming to a stop, stood upon the brilliant green carpet figured with writhing dragons that they had bought on their honeymoon in Hong Kong. As she looked up at the open gallery, she could see the bookcases full of the books she loved, her desk. How many hours had she spent up there reading, reading, writing, studying, pining for a love she would never have here, trying to appease her loneliness with her studies, with the company of people and their ideas, within the pages of her books? That was the room that had saved her, saved her and helped her escape to a world where she felt at home with her imaginary companions, learning from and exploring other minds as her own grew in response to theirs.

A mind that is stretched to a new idea, never returns to its original dimension.

This was a room where learning was meant to be fostered, not stifled, growth encouraged, not confined, this room had been her soulmate, encouraging her to stretch her mind and feed upon all that it had to give her. This room had nourished her; it had not taken anything from her.

Every step the mind takes in its progress towards knowledge makes some discovery, which is not only new, but, the best too, for that time at least.

She walked out of the room, went to the front door and lowered the lever to open it. One door, two doors, shut behind her, the female face and the male stoically staring at her departing back, both of them guarding entry, separate and strong, each in their own manner. She picked her way over the flagstones she had laboriously hauled, pushed and pulled into place, moving to the small gates of iron whorls and arabesques that separated the garden from the entrance. She shut the gate and began to walk up the hill. She looked to her right, at the meandering gravel pathway winding over the stony ground, at the pattern and proportion of the plants she had selected. They were growing, as she had imagined they would, into a green pattern of leaves and trunks that looked as though they had evolved and found their place of their own accord, instead of being part of a planting, a contrived though harmonious pattern. She turned and looked to her left.

Concetto: the mental image formed by the artist before beginning work.

The curving wall of terra cotta coloured plaster separated the greeny-grey leaves of the olive trees into a "bosco." Her symmetrical planting of the trees was a tribute to her personal history. The olive orchard she had planted didn't look very different from the groves of trees she had first seen on her father's farms on the island in Greece at the age of eleven, this rocky terrain and the undulating, shimmery sea of silver green her personal, living, recreation of her heritage.

The garden is a representation of Paradise— "a place of peace, light, and beauty, echoing the primordial perfection of nature."

The gates loomed in front of her. They were elegant, imposing and beautiful. How many times had she entered and departed through their portals as they slowly opened and then closed behind her? They physically marked part of her life with an indelibly intertwined emotional link. How had she arrived here in this land, in this house? She knew now that she had chosen this path in emulation of her parent's own immigration. She had never questioned that she wasn't meant to live in Vancouver all of her life. She had thought it the most natural thing in the world to go and live two thousand miles away from her family at the age of twenty, to move to a little town on the border with Mexico, to choose a life of change over that of the familiar. She had wanted to have a family, and she had. She had wanted to grow, to challenge herself with new horizons everyday, and she had. She had wanted to love, passionately, completely, oblivious to the consequences, and she had. She didn't know what drew her to the gates, to walk through them and look down the hill at this metaphor of a life she was leaving behind, she just knew that it was her time. This was part of who she was meant to be and where she was supposed to go. Everything she had created had been a new version of the portrait hanging on the living room wall. That woman was her as the artist had seen her; her creations were her as she saw herself. And she wasn't done yet.

Her evolution wasn't over. She would never outlive the need to express her conceptions in something physical, an exterior expression of herself so that others could partake of what she saw in her mind's eye and share in the beauty of contrast; there is no black without white, there is no shadow without light, there is no sadness without joy. Others would see that she couldn't live her life without acknowledging that her time was finite and that her life deserved to be lived to the fullest while she had a place on earth. Her family and this home she had created were just part of the mosaic she would call her own, with all the myriad colours and shades of experience. Her life was never meant to be a lifeless, monochromatic blur, but rather a vibrant mix of brilliant hues. Her life, all life, was meant to be brilliant colour, brilliant colour blending to form a blinding light.

We must be the change we wish to see in the world.

APPENDIX

PRELUDE

Chapter One THE MANTLEPIECE

14 .... Rene Descartes
14 .... Mark Twain

Chapter Two **THE PHOTOGRAPH**
17 .... William Shakespeare
18 .... John Dryden
20 .... Albert Einstein
22 .... Bernard Williams
23 .... George Eliot
23 .... Victor Hugo
24 .... Benjamin Franklin
25 .... Rei Kawakubo
29 .... Royal Museum, Victoria, British Columbia

Chapter Three **THE RING**
34 .... Adrian Randolph
35 .... William Shakespeare
37 .... Adrian Randolph
38 .... ibid
38 .... John Milton
39 .... Cherubino da Spoleto

Chapter Four **THE BATHING SUIT**
45 .... Bernadette Spinoza
47 .... Joseph Heller
48 .... Bible, Proverbs
48 .... unknown
49 .... Jonathon Edwards
49 .... Oscar Wilde

Chapter Five **THE CANDLESTICKS**
55 .... Zen Saying
55 .... Arnold Geulinx
56 .... M.J. Kondwani
58 .... unknown
59 .... Lawrence Hill

Chapter Six **THE MEMENTO**
63 .... George Santayaya
65 .... Victor Hugo

183 .... Samuel Taylor Coleridge
184 .... Ernst Hans Gombrich
184 .... William Shakespeare
185 .... Ernst Hans Gombrich
185 .... ibid
186 .... Swartz
186 .... Fairy Tales Grimm
187 .... Alanus
187 .... Ralph Waldo Emerson

Chapter Sixteen THE MONEY

192 .... Plato
193 .... Victor Hugo
193 .... Therapist
193 .... George Bernard Shaw
194 .... Mary Astell
195 .... Albert Einstein
195 .... Matchbox Twenty
196 .... Ahad Ha-am
197 .... Lawrence Hill
198 .... Jean Jaques Rousseau
200 .... Albert Einstein
201 .... Samuel Johnson
205 .... Lawrence Hill
206 .... Zines
207 .... e.e. cummings
207 .... M. Scott Peck, M.D.
209 .... Thucidides
210 .... Dido
210 .... Thucidides
211 .... Zines
211 .... Dolores Ibarruri
212 .... William Shakespeare
213 .... ibid
213 .... Victor Hugo
213 .... Mary Astell
214 .... Elizabeth De Bold
214 .... Arnold Whittick

Chapter Seventeen THE BODY

217 .... Epedocles
218 .... Jean Paul Sartre
218 .... Lawrence Hill

BIOGRAPHY

Konstantina was born in Vancouver, B.C. to Greek immigrant parents. While studying towards a degree in Latin American Literature— the first student to do so at the University of British Columbia— she married and moved to Nogales, Arizona to begin a family. Later she followed her husband farther south to Culiacan, Mexico, where for five years she raised two sons while studying interior design by correspondence from the New York School of Interior Design.

The family moved back to Arizona and welcomed a daughter as Konstantina began her design business, Mahlia Interiors, and started construction on a home that was her calling card as a designer. Mahlia Furniture Collection evolved from the need to furnish her home, and her jewelry collection grew soon after.

Konstantina returned to school, and graduated from the University of Arizona with both English and University Honours in May of 2003. She received a second degree from the Eller Entrepreneurship Program in May 2004 while finishing *The House of Many Faces*, published that same summer.